D|

Insta.... Actions

The Muslim Mind Training Manual
Think of it as 'antivirus software for the mind'.

Thanks are due to again to Mufti Ismail Menk for bringing this book to peoples' attention, and the support of the Ummah for the success of my previous book, all of whose support has been so fundamental and generous.

This book is published as a vigorous response to the call for strength and courage when facing the many changes that we have had to face in 2020. It is all of the finest techniques about how to help one's mind to thrive easily and without fuss, inshallah.
 Praise for Instant Insights, the previous book:

"Very few books marry the Islamic aspects with the medical aspects of mental health. I recommend this book very highly."

- Mufti Menk, March 2020

Special thanks are also due to Z @liftmeupdaily

First Edition Published April 2020.

Oxford, UK.

www.drtkharris.wordpress.com

CustomID-PP-112125778-o/f/b-10101975

drtkharris@gmail.com
drtkharris.wordpress.com

 drtkharris

Instant
Actions

*To empower all Muslims facing difficulties, doing their best.
You are my brothers, sister, fathers, and mothers.*

*For my parents, my brothers, and their families,
for their unbelievable and unwavering support.*

For my wife and children.

And above all, for the sake of Allah.

Issues

Actions

INSTANT ACTIONS

Bismillahir-Rahmaanir-Raheem.
In the name of Allah, the Beneficent, the Merciful.

I write this while wishing I could have a conversation with you. Who are you, I wonder? What made you come to read this? You could be a Muslim, looking to remind yourself for reasons to be happy. You could be a non-Muslim, intrigued as to how this very serious religion, so often depicted negatively by some media, could possibly have happy devotees.

What I have to tell you is going to make you understand, and I hope you it will make you smile too, Inshallah. The real reason I would like to talk to you is because we could have a conversation. You could corner me and really interrogate what I have say. Then I would be more certain that you come away convinced. In the absence of our meeting, these words will have to do.

The Islamic world used to be a pioneer in medicine and mental health. The world's first psychiatric ward, in fact, was established in Baghdad, Iraq in 705CE by a doctor called Al-Razi. He believed strongly that mental disorders were medical conditions, and his treatments included talking therapies and physical agents such as calming potions, restorative foods, recreation, and occupation. After this period, Islam lost this tradition somewhat, for a great many years.

When the Ottoman Empire was losing its power, it is thought the Muslim powers of the day believed that they were being punished for their scientific progress. They would of course have been deeply mistaken, but nonetheless it could explain why we entered a darkness of times when we reverted back to suspicion of evidence and intellect, mislabelling anything new as blasphemous. We lost the ability to tell the difference between meaningless bid'ah and genuine medical advancement.

All major religions have been through such phases in their history. Allah knows best why these things happened, but now the Islamic world is regaining its confidence and restoring the practice of combining spiritual with scientific. A young man studying to be an Alim in the holy city of Medina itself will have no problem getting help with his mental health, should he need it, through both spiritual and medical channels, with full integration of the two ways. Alhamdulillah.

So, to the matter at hand. Instant Actions will give you a refreshed attitude to your happiness. But we need to understand how important attitude is. Let's start with a very important, and maybe controversial point. Happiness doesn't have very much to do with where you are, or what happened to you. Allow me to set out my case with a story.

In southern Sudan in the early days Islamic Empire, Chief Khalid had two handsome sons- twins, in fact who were coming of age in the next month. It was customary to give young men presents to celebrate the event. But Khalid had a problem. He had no idea what to get for his two sons, because they were so very peculiar, and so very different from one another.

The first twin, Umar, was an eternal optimist. No matter what happened, he always saw the bright side. It was lucky that he was still alive, for it was every other week that he would go off on some risky hunting adventure or other. His mother was terrified he would never come back, but by sheer luck, he always did. "Surely his luck will run out soon." Chief Khalid thought to himself.

The second twin, Saud, was a the opposite of Umar. Saud was a pessimist. You know, his glass was always half empty. He never dared to do anything adventurous, and sat around being sad all the time because he worried that something would always go wrong.

One day the two sons sat in their sunlit palace dining room, discussing the upcoming ceremony. "I bet Father's gifts for us will be wonderful!" said Umar to Saud, "I am so looking forward to getting mine, aren't you?"

"No way" replied Saud, "mine will definitely be worse than yours. Whatever he gets me I bet it will be of no good".

The Chief overheard them as he listened from nearby. He anticipated his sons' reactions; he had, after all, seen them grow up. He was tired of their apparent entrenched attitudes, and wanted to wanted to make a last ditch attempt to change each boy's extreme views on life. It was, after all, the eve of their transition to manhood. They were becoming men, leaders, and one of them would be Chief one day.

Chief Khalid retired to his palace chamber and puffed on his hookah pipe, thinking long and hard. How could one disappoint an eternal optimist? And at the other extreme, how could one make a pessimist smile? After a while, it came to him. A most cunning plan! He would give them coming-of-age gifts that would force the change.

To the overly happy soul Umar, he would give a gift of such abject humiliation that it would make anyone doubt their life's worth. To the pessimist, Saud, he would give something so wonderful that Saud wouldn't be able to deny a sense of joy.

So, for Saud, Chief Khalid decided instructed his traders and merchants to acquire a wonderful horse. Not just any horse. He had them obtain an *Akhal Teke-* a golden-skinned blonde horse of exceptional intelligence and beauty, reared only on the steppes of Asia. Within a few weeks, his people had managed to source the animal from a contact in the Mongol Empire.

When it came, it was clear that this horse was swift and strong and in the peak of its health. It was so beautiful that people came from surrounding villages just to see it.

For Umar, the Chief had another, much less charming present planned. He had his servants gather all of the horse dung they could find, and make it up into a pile. He was going to give his optimistic son a big pile of stinking horse manure. "Surely that would make Umar climb down from his evergreen palm tree," the Chief thought.

The day came for the ceremony, and the townspeople gathered in the square to witness the grand coming-of-age ritual. The two sons stood proudly on either side of their father. They were both dressed in gleaming attire: ornately decorated warrior uniforms, accompanied by shields, axes and spears. They spent the morning watching various showmen and travelling entertainers. The crowd were entertained by displays of power, athletic prowess, dexterity and artistry.

Then, after a grand lunch, attention turned to the two sons. It was time for the Chief to give them their gifts. The first was Saud. A fanfare of beating drums announced its arrival. Led my two guardsmen, the horse emerged into the square from one of the stone arches, where it had been shrouded under a silken red blanket. As it appeared, the blanket fluttered off its back, landing gently onto the shiny marble floor, and the horse trotted around the space, its hide glinting metallic gold in the afternoon sun. What a sight! It drew cries of amazement and cheers from the crowd.

Eyes then turned to Saud the great pessimist. On seeing his beautiful new horse, Saud immediately fell into floods of tears. These were not tears of happiness. Saud seemed inconsolably disappointed. Everyone was flabbergasted. How could he be upset by such a magnificent thing?

"What's wrong, son? This is the greatest horse in all the land!" said his father.

"I know, Father," replied Saud, "but look at how handsome it is! Horses only live for limited years, but humans live up to seventy! It is just so sad that one day this horse will die, and it will break my heart when this happens!! Why would you punish me so?". And with that, Saud turned and ran sobbing back into the palace.

Chief Khalid shook his head in despair. It really did seem that nothing would make his pessimistic son happy. Still, he could hope at least to turn the mind of his opposite number, so next came Umar's turn.

He turned to face Umar, but this son had disappeared off somewhere in all the commotion.

A manservant came along to the Chief and breathlessly declared, "Chief, Chief, I beg of thee, come quickly! Umar has found his gift and lost his mind!"

Chief Khalid thought the worst; surely this terrible gift was a step too far! What if Umar would have discovered the pile of horse dung and gone insane?! Khaled and his two aides rushed along to the stables, where the horse dung, and its new owner Umar, were to be found.

They were greeted by a remarkable sight. The pile of horse manure was as high as a horse itself, and on top of it, knee deep, was Umar. He was wildly playing and digging about in the black mound, like a child in fresh snow. He wasn't upset at all. In fact, he seemed to be overjoyed! He didn't even notice his father walk in.

"Son! Come down from there! Why are you so happy with this gift?!'"

Umar looked up and shouted in glee, "Because there is surely a horse somewhere in this pile, father!!"

Chief Khalid shook his head. Imagine that! The young warrior was so optimistic that he believed that there was a living horse hiding in that unsightly, stinking mess. Of course, there wasn't a horse in there. But Umar seemed happy anyway. The truth is, even if he carried on digging around and found no horse, he would probably still be happy somehow. True to his character, he was a tireless, endless optimist.

Why did I tell you this story? Well, as Muslims we have a direct line to Allah, and he has given us endless reassurances that we can be happy. This is our very special privilege as people of Islam. It teaches us that happiness is a steady state of contentment and ease, with the ability to experience both joy and pain without either being the story of our life. Happiness comes from the inside.

My last book, Instant Insights, described how the mind works and how one can use this knowledge to understand and work towards contentment and success. The book in your hand now is more focussed on training the mind using this knowledge. If the last book was about computer sciences, this book is about how to program your computer.

I have, as I did in Instant Insights, married the scientific with the religious guidance in mental health and wellbeing.

However, let's be clear that Muslim does not require science, and science does not have authority over faith. Science is evolving, being rewritten and refreshed all the time, while the Quran does not need even a single letter changed.

Reliability of a Hadith, and reliable interpretations of the Quran, have been my great allies in this effort, and I thank Allah for helping me along by giving me the chance to ask some great scholars as to what they think of this or that matter in the book.

The Quran is irrefutable, and every copy is identical, syllable for syllable, in its original Arabic. This does not mean that it is always easy to interpret. Allah states in the Quran that within it are words that are clear, and others which will become clear at their appointed time, and still others which will remain a mystery. He goes on to state that people will interpret its words for their own ends, sometimes correctly, sometimes incorrectly, for both righteous and nefarious reasons. I hope to minimise such mistakes by sticking to quotes and references which are clear and universally agreed interpretation.

May Allah, and my brothers and sisters forgive me if I have made any errors, and as always, get in touch to let me have your views and thoughts on what would help you next.

Anyway, where were we? Oh yes. What power does our circumstance have over our happiness? Nothing. We can't choose our circumstances. What matters is what we make of them. This book will prove why you can, and should, find reasons to smile every single day.

T K Harris
April 2020
Sha'baan 1441 AH

The Muslim mind at its best

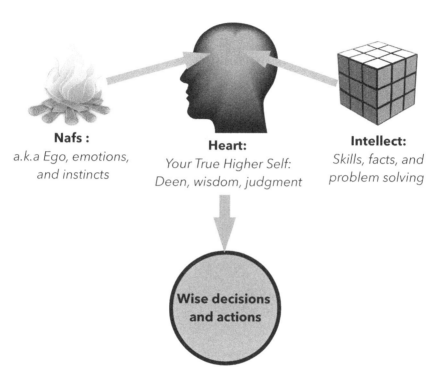

Nafs :
a.k.a Ego, emotions, and instincts

Heart:
Your True Higher Self: Deen, wisdom, judgment

Intellect:
Skills, facts, and problem solving

Wise decisions and actions

1

**While others have wishes,
the Muslim has a purpose.**

When We Lose Sight of Our Purpose

The Muslim believes that Allah has not made him as a coincidence. The purpose of existence for all Muslims, at its core, is to *worship* and *know* God. In parallel with this main purpose, we have Earthly purposes too.

Now, having purposes is extremely important for a human being. Let's look at the components of well-being as science defines it.

This is called a 'wellbeing box':

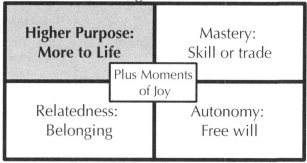

I've highlighted the box relevant to this chapter. Scientists have been trying to define 'wellbeing' for some years now, but one part they can all agree on is a sense of higher purpose. If you know why you are on earth, then you can walk tall with a sense of direction and confidence. There are few things that can get in the way of a person who has adopted a purpose.

So, we start off with a very powerful straightforward exercise. Clarify your Purposes.

Clarify your purposes

Purpose is divided into Roles and Goals:

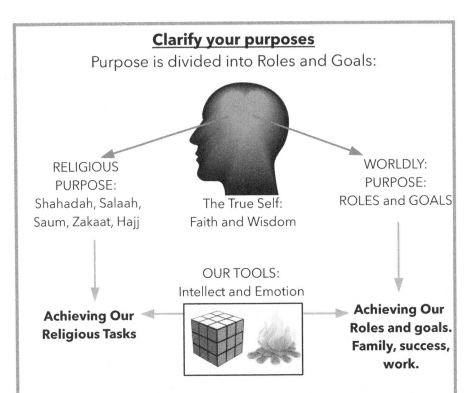

RELIGIOUS
PURPOSE:
Shahadah, Salaah,
Saum, Zakaat, Hajj

The True Self:
Faith and Wisdom

WORLDLY:
PURPOSE:
ROLES and GOALS

OUR TOOLS:
Intellect and Emotion

**Achieving Our
Religious Tasks**

**Achieving Our
Roles and goals.
Family, success,
work.**

a. Make a list of your *religious goals/ tasks* for the day.
b. Make a list of the **roles you have at home**. (Brother, etc)
c. Do the same for the **roles you have at work.** (Boss, etc)
d. The same for your **social life.** (Game team member etc)
e. Make a list of your **goals for yourself-** educationally, work wise etc.

Look through the list. Appreciate that you have quite a complex life. Be kind to yourself; appreciate that it is difficult. Pray to Allah that he reminds you of these things.

Now come up with **one idea for each item** in which you could easily do that thing a little bit better, starting today. If you have a day planner, make a to-do list of tasks for this and start doing it.

Use this space for your own notes on the exercise opposite.

Grief is love, expressed in tears.
The Muslim who does not grieve, hardly exists.
Grief is itself a medicine,
Grief is Historian of the Heart.

Adjusting to a Sudden Loss or Change

Change, and loss, welcome or unwelcome, are part of life. The mental consequences even of a dramatic positive change can be terribly confusing or painful, feeling like madness even. However, we are to know that the reaction to sudden change or loss is, for most people, a period of difficult but normal psychological adjustment.

'Be sure we shall test you with something of fear and hunger, some loss in goods, lives and the fruits of your toil, but give glad tiding to those who patiently persevere. Who say, when afflicted with calamity: To Allah we belong, and to him is our return' (Quran: 62).

Here are ten of the most stressful changes, as measured by psychological impact, that people feel.

- Major Injury or Illness (Fears or events)
- Death of a spouse
- Marital separation or divorce
- Loss of Job or income
- The death of a close family member
- The early part of marriage
- Moving House
- Retirement
- Transitioning to adulthood roles
- A traumatic accident or experience

This is not a complete list. Also, different changes affect different people, differently.

I remember once helping an Arab prince who was deeply distressed. He had great wealth, including aeroplanes, houses and more than a hundred thoroughbred horses, but one day, the first horse he ever had, died. He was inconsolable, and felt his world was collapsing. Alhamdulillah, with some minor pointers and reassurance, he adjusted and moved forward.

Adjustment to any major change goes through a number of well-described stages. The stages can be mixed up in their length, order and severity. It's called the DABDA model:

Denial:
Refusal to acknowledge the change has happened.
It's not happening. It's a mistake. Needless to worry.

Anger:
Why me? Whose fault was this? Not mine!

Bargaining:
Irrational hope.
I will improve Allah, I promise! Just undo this problem!

Depressive phase:
a) Reactive: *I am so sad that this has happened*
b) Preparatory: *Life is going to be very different*

Acceptance:
Ok, this is my new reality.

As a rule of thumb, 80% of adjustments have completed successfully by three months, and 96% by six months. The remaining 4% could be where the troubles are becoming long term, leading to or resulting from issues such as depression, further decline in circumstances, addiction, or other complications.

Adjustment to change is not an illness, nor abnormal: it is part of the normal psychological experience for most people in life.

Where grief over a death is concerned, it is not unusual to find some people wishing to be alongside their loved one. This is sometimes mistaken for suicidality, which is not the case. It is part of some peoples' grieving process. Some people also report seeing or hearing their loved one, especially in quiet times. This is also not abnormal.

Islam spells it out, doesn't it?

Allahu Akbar, it does. Every event in the Muslim's life is written for them far before they were even born. Using free will to live out their destiny as best they can in the course of finding God, living within their limitations, is the only thing a Muslim really has to do.

Muslims are of course permitted and expected to cry and express grief over losses and deaths. Islam encourages Muslims to talk about and remember lost loved ones and recall the good deeds of their life, as part of a helpful positive appreciation process, to reflect on the good times

9

and qualities of the person. It is reported that Prophet PBUH himself never forgot his love for his beloved wife, Khadijah, even years after her death.

The Seerah of the Prophet PBUH record numerous instances of how he approached everyday occurrences. Stories abound for how he would frown upon those who spend too much time regretting things of the past, or dominated by excess guilt.

So with the next exercise, we will look at how to deal with a change effectively.

Instagram, March 2020

Mind Training Session: Deal With A Change Effectively

You are going to go through the DABDA stages. The Nafs (Ego and Emotions) are very upset when change happens. If they are not tended to, we find adjustment even harder than we need to. So, we can look at helping do the **emotional work** of accepting the change, as **T-E-A-R:**

Try to accept the reality of the change

Experience the pain of the change, just let it happen

Adjust to the new environment

Reinvest yourself in the new reality

You can't necessarily rush the emotional work. However, what you can do is stand aside when the emotions of change (DABDA) are afoot. Give yourself time. Pray to Allah for humility and patience. **Reinvestment is the most proactive part.** You have the choice to reconstruct yourself or your environment in a proactive way, with optimism and energy. Pain of loss and change does not disappear completely, but it does fade, and many a person has emerged much stronger after experiencing the unexpected.

Use this space for your own notes on the exercise opposite.

**Allah has designed Time
to pass by us without consent.**

**Time is like the wind;
it lifts the light-hearted,
and leaves the heavy.**

Days Blurring Into One Another.

When we find ourselves adrift with too much to do, or the opposite, with nothing to do, we can lose sight of ourselves.

If you fail to plan, they say, you plan to fail. So much of our unhappiness comes from the fact that we know what to do, but we don't do what we know. Life becomes a series of unaccomplished days, and a few years later, we wonder where the time went.

If some of us were to truly take account of all the time that we lose unwisely, it is mind-boggling. If we employed a firm but fair personal trainer who was to take over our life and spent all our time with us making us actually do what we intended, we would astound ourselves with how much we could accomplish.

So, how do we claim back some sense of progress and clarity? We hang our days on **structure,** and **variety.** The next exercise looks at just such a plan, in a small way of claiming some of that focus back.

Imposing structure: make concrete, doable days.

This lasts for one month. It will improve your contentment in several ways, along with helping you learn about yourself.

Get yourself a diary, or a notebook. A page per day. Mark out the five salah times on each page, for each day, for the coming month. See next page for an example.

Every morning before or after Fajr, spend ten minutes writing whatever you want. Let it flow out. Anything that comes to mind, just write it. Doodle or scribble. One word or a hundred, it's fine.
Then, write out a to do list. Put an item in between each salah time, wherever it make the most sense. There are four types of thing. Ideally, each day should have one of each:
Something new and challenging.
Something that makes someone in your family smile.
Something that is good fun, just in the moment.
Something that is boring but important.

In the evening, write down what you did, how it went, and what you are thankful for. That's your page done. Do this every day for a month. Watch how things change. Thank me later. If you find it useful to carry on beyond a month, do so.

Extra power moves:
a) Increase your dhikr (remembrance and reflection of God) during this time because it boosts your short term memory-crucial in helping to get clarity back.

b) Consider increasing your fresh fruit intake too, and foods rich in Vitamin B such as beans and brown bread.

daily planner DATE:

Fajr

6AM

Learn Islamic
History
1 hour online

7AM

8AM

9AM

10AM

11AM

12PM

Zuhr

1PM

Get Mum
flowers

2PM

Asr

3PM

Play Scrabble
with Asif

4PM

5PM

Maghrib

6PM

Clean the
garage

7PM

8PM

I'sha

9PM

10PM

11PM

3 MOST IMPORTANT TASKS

1. Get groceries!
2. Ring TK Paints Ltd
3. Cancel bus ticket

Types of task each day must have

New and/or
challenging

Make a loved one
smile

Good fun thing

Boring but
important

Achieved? Comments

17

Look at the example on the previous page and try the same for
yourself here.. Pencil in as much as you wish. Start small!!

daily planner

DATE:

| | 3 MOST IMPORTANT TASKS |
6AM

7AM

8AM

9AM

| NOTES |
10AM

11AM

12PM

1PM

2PM

3PM

4PM

5PM

6PM

7PM

8PM

9PM

10PM

11PM

Being Unsure of Our Worth

The Muslim is told that he is the Highest of all God's earthly creations. The Muslim also believes that God's views of things are final. We are guided as to what to seek or not seek, to like and not like, by His command.

In the Quran, when Allah created Man, the angels themselves bowed down to Man as a sign of how highly Man is regarded by God.

So, we know that God values us very highly indeed, just as we are. We know this for a fact. Wouldn't it be foolish for us to disagree with Him on this point?

So, we have to like.. ourselves? For what reason though?

Not just like. Love. You are asking about self-worth. Your self worth need not have any reason at all. Muslims have self worth which is **unconditional**. We must believe that as human beings, we are worthy and of great value just as we are, without needing to do a single thing.

But aren't we supposed to have a purpose? To fulfil some kind of journey, a series of good deeds, to have worth?

We are all created with some kind of purpose in mind, you are correct. But at its very base, part of that purpose might just be to just exist, even if it is for a few flickers of life before death. Our existence on Earth, each as individuals, is

19

not a coincidence. We are worthy, even as we just live and breathe.

It is extremely helpful to keep this in mind when you doubt your belief in yourself. Indeed, any person who adopts unconditional self worth is far more optimistic and successful in their approach to anything in life.

Doesn't self worth come from achievement too?

No, although I understand why you ask that. We gain *satisfaction* from achievement, not *self worth*. There's a subtle but very important difference. It's OK to be dissatisfied with yourself if you haven't achieved much, but it is unwise to ever have low self worth. Self worth is that bit of you that is inside, saying that you are an OK and a good person no matter what you achieve or fail. It's about having the biggest part of you feeling OK regardless of whatever good or bad things happen in your life. That makes for stability and dignity.

Wouldn't that lead to arrogance and an air of superiority?

Self worth must exist alongside humility. Arrogance and an air of superiority happen when you believe your worth is greater than someone else's. This is the insecurity of the Nafs. Muslims acknowledge the Nafs, and indeed we use the Nafs, but we don't follow its direction blindly. We are not distracted by the petty wish of having high status or being better than others.

We are all to regard each other as equal, except in matters of closeness to Allah, which is up to God to judge. Only God's judgment could ever decide if one has greater value than the other, and this happens when he looks at what is in our Heart. The depth and breadth of our Heart is something we can work on, but it is only fully visible to Him.

If we value ourselves like this, aren't we in danger of never seeing where we need to improve? Won't we fail to try hard if we just feel so relaxed about everything?

On the contrary. Think about how the Nafs works. It's like a fire inside you: it can warm you, prompting you to act, but that is enough. Staying near it overheats you, and the fire goes from being a tool to a hazard.

When you feel inadequate, that is the Nafs telling you so; the insecurity comes about because you believe you have lower status than someone else,, you're insecure about your ability, and you worry that something will go wrong or that you will fail.

The Nafs is like a fire.
It can warm you, but it can burn you too.

Fear might make you focus on a problem but it only really works in emergencies: you can do something quickly to deal with a change.

If you rely on fear or intense anxiety for your normal, everyday way of thinking, you become tired, weary and cynical about everything. You fail more often because your mind is not as creative or composed when you are in this state. And even if you do succeed, you get carried away with success for a short time, only to become freshly fearful of the next thing, or arrogant and dismissive of it.

The key to improvement is a much more calm approach. You listen to your emotions, because they are your Nafs (Ego's) anxieties, and thank Allah for them, because they give you a starting point. From then on, though, it is your Heart and your Intellect which take over. Your Heart tells you that you are worthy, and that you must act humbly, and the Intellect goes about trying to find ways to find solutions to whatever challenge you face, in a sober, matter-of-fact, everyday way.

If you have trouble accepting yourself, well, accept that too! Understand that you hope to accept yourself, but that at the moment it isn't easy. Accept that it will come in its own time, and ask Allah to help you towards that goal. *Claim* yourself!

If you have done something awful and feel unforgivable, then that's fine too. Ask Allah for forgiveness and be sincere in resolving to not do the thing again. If you are sincere, he will forgive you.

You might not even feel strong in yourself. You might even worry that though you don't want to repeat the offence, you might still fall for temptation at a weak moment.

It doesn't matter. Focus on right now. For now, you really don't want to do it, and you sincerely hope not to do it again. That is enough. God will forgive you every time, as long as you resolve not to repeat it sincerely each time. This is your way out.

If you do repeat the pattern, look at where and when it happens and try to avoid that situation. If you can't beat the pattern despite your reasonable efforts, seek help.

Some things you can't easily fix yourself at all. They may be a sign of mental illness. Examples are things like being stuck in rut of hopelessness, being addicted to any substance or behaviour, and mental situations where you feel like a burden, racked with guilt, with a very poor view of yourself, and you feel unable to prevent a terrible future.

Allah commands us to look after our minds and bodies properly, and to seek help if either of these become unwell. Seek help from a doctor, or confide in someone whom you know and trust, such as a kindly Imam, a close friend, or trusted relative. There may be helplines and agencies in your area which are also dedicated towards people who are struggling in this way. Use them. There is no shame in taking control of a situation by calling in some outside help.

Mind Training Session: Self acceptance

Remember these points:
- God is always close by, and always ready to listen.
- Feeling worthy on the inside protects against feeling terrible when bad things happen.
- It's OK to feel bad: just let it pass without judging yourself.

Steps

1. Imagine, or remember, a time when someone you cared for felt really bad about themselves. They could have been overcome with guilt, difficult to console. Imagine you are at your best self. What could you

a) say to them?

b) do with them?

c) do for them?

Write down some ideas or think them through.

2. Now think about times when you feel bad about yourself or are struggling.

How do you typically respond to yourself in these situations? Please write down what you typically do, what you say, and note the tone in which you talk to yourself.

Did you notice a difference? If so, then recognise this fact: treat yourself as if you are your own 'loved one'. How would you console yourself in future?

You are loved by Allah in great abundance.
Treat yourself in a way that respects this truth!

Use this space for your own notes on the exercise opposite.

**The Muslim with Akhlaaq
has learned the art of choosing his real thoughts.
His principles are made both from iron bars
and delicate sacrifices.**

A Lack of Rules or Habits: *Akhlaaq*

Everyday life is best approached by being both proactive and reactive.

Proactively, we set out doing our routine or our to-do list.

Reactively, we deal with things that come up and interrupt our plans for better or worse.

It can seem hard to know how to be consistent, and which path to take. Being too proactive means we are rigidly stuck with our plans, and risk neglecting new opportunities or dangers. Being too reactive means we lose track and feel aimless.

What would help us to be more consistent in any situation?

Islam is all about wisdoms, rules and consolations about daily life. We just need to distil them and apply them. This is what leads us to the idea of Akhlaaq.

Akhlaaq basically means character, personality, disposition.
It is a broad impression of how a person conducts themselves. People with good Akhlaaq seem to be unfazed by things, as if neither good nor bad event could upset or surprise them. They have a sort of 'aura' of serenity and wisdom that underpins a wonderful persona. People want to be around those who have good Akhlaaq.

The Muslim faces life like anyone else. We experience emotions and we react to things like anyone else. Akhlaaq are facts and beliefs which are immensely useful to navigate life.

In a person with good Akhlaaq, manners and wisdoms prevail in their reactions to any news, and in their everyday behaviour. They seem to float above disappointments and sail through torment more easily, because they always hold certain beliefs in the front of their mind. Akhlaaq are like 'Rules of engagement' for everyday life. A person with good Akhlaaq still has pain and dilemmas, but these are dealt with in a more 'routine' way because Akhlaaq is rules for how to be at all times. It's a formula for dealing with everything in a humble, accepting, way, showing consistently good qualities such as inner strength, wisdom, hope, dignity, direction and good humour.

Akhlaaq comes in two parts: **Truths**, and **Conduct**. The next two chapters will describe these in more detail, and the Training Sessions will help you to draw up your own desirable Akhlaaq system.

Difficulty facing Realities of Life

Let's deal with the first: the Truths of Life.

Truths are facts. Facts are always good, in the end. Having useful truths close to your Heart is like a fortification around your conduct, a defence against making big mistakes.

The truth is a fortification around your Heart/ True Self

The Quran makes no promises that we get to see God's justice and wisdom immediately. God states that he may even bless ignorant people with wealth, and that they will mistake this for being loved by God. So we are not to look at what others have, to make any conclusions about how God sees them.

The Muslim is told that he will be duly rewarded for goodness, but that this may not be apparent immediately or in a way that he has asked. The nature of the reward is up to God. Further, if bad things happen to him, the Muslim is also told that he must not take them as signs of being punished. Again, punishments and bad experiences may happen, but the Muslim is not to know what is and what isn't such.

29

By looking at all these rules and drawing them together, the Muslim gets a set of 'Life Truths'. I've made my own list here, for example:

- **Life on earth seems unfair**. We do not know why Allah permitted a bad thing to happen, but we believe there is something in it that is better for us. We move forward without resentment or confusion.
- **Bad things happen to good people**, and good things happen to bad people. We cannot see Allah's reasons.
- **Not everything will seem to work out**. Our prayers will seem unanswered; we must accept this with a steady hand and a thankful heart, and make our efforts nonetheless.
- **Everything in life is temporary**: good times, and bad times, don't last forever.
- **Expectations in life are always changing.** We must adapt, not get infuriated.
- **People lie, and deceive, and people act selfishly.** We might spot this sometimes, or we might not. So be it.
- **We cannot get along with everyone**. We will be disappointed, and we will disappoint others. We move on.
- **The results of our efforts are up to Allah.** Our job is to just make our efforts as best we can.
- **The present time is the only time** anyone has control over. It is the only time when we do anything to define ourselves.

Those sound like quite difficult things to accept! But I can see how they are helpful.

Indeed. Islam is very realistic about how to approach life on Earth. These truths settle the mind.

God does exercise ultimate morality on earth, and people always get their due, whether in this life or the hereafter. However, the Muslim is told that God's justice and reasons are outside his perception, so he is not to seek them out hoping for some kind of fairytale life. So we take things as they are, as apparently fair or not, broken or not, knowing quite plainly that God's wisdom is far greater than ours.

The next exercise will help you to draw out some truths that will come in handy for when you face difficulty, and equally, they will keep you humble when you are feeling blessed. Truths keep us on an even keel, neither too upset by disaster not too giddy when we are victorious. Being to exuberant when times are good can lead us to feel arrogant, or worse, it could lead to incurring jealousy and ill will from other people.

Enjoy the good times and be saddened by the bad times, but don't overdo your reaction to either. It is better to stay tethered to a place of moderation.

Set out, and live by, helpful Truths

A. Set up a list of truths.

Reflect on good and bad times in your life. How long did they last? What kind of things would you say to yourself when you were younger, that would help you get through those times more effectively? Read through Hadith or Quran in your language, and find verses or saying that illustrate the reality of how life on Earth unfolds for us.

Look back two pages at the list of truths I drew up. They were, and still are, helpful to me. I am sure that many of them will be helpful to you too. Add or amend to those.

B. Keep the Truths close to your Heart.

This is done by repetition, enrichment, and application.

Repetition is where you keep the list written close to you, and read it over frequently. In the morning, or evening, or after a meal. Have it on your phone, or as a voice recording.

Enrichment is when you read Quran and contemplate its meaning, and when you discuss and share your Truths with people you love and trust, and reinforce them when you make your dhikr and du'aa (remembrance and prayer).

Application is when you face any event, joyous or sad, and look through your Truths to find meaning and relevance.

Use this space for your own notes on the exercise opposite.

Many are wise enough to know what to do next.
Be the Muslim who actually does it.

Poor Conduct or Reputation

Conduct is about how a person *ought to behave*. People work towards goals in life but they lose sight of their conduct, becoming ruthless or deceptive or ignoring other important things in the pursuit of their prize.

Islam's solution? Islam says the methods, way in which we do things, are always important. The Muslim has goals too, but above any 'fixed' goals he is told to have 'goals of conduct'. These are collection of ways in how he should live his life, in an ongoing, everyday way. Achievement of the goal comes second to how you go about achieving it.

The Quran and Hadith are overflowing with examples, rules and stories showing how one should carry out one's affairs. On the ground, these translate as 'principles to live by'. Principles are universal, steady, and they add a golden colour to your life because they are like graceful adornments of your Akhlaaq. The Muslim reminds himself of these principles every day, by reading Quran and Hadith. In my last book, Instant Insights, I had gathered a large number of rules for everyday conduct just from the Quran.

To make Conduct meaningful and easier to apply to your life, you have to focus on things which play to your strengths as a person, and things which you find are absolutely essential for you to be. If you become very old, inshallah, you would look back on your life and be proud of having conducted yourself in these given ways.

So with that in mind, here is an example list of Conduct rules

"I will try to be..
- **Thankful.** To thank Allah for what I have, knowing what others less fortunate me don't have.
- **Hopeful.** To keep optimism and hope always in mind. It gets me through difficulty, and conquers fear.
- **Purposeful.** To take on tasks and goals which improve my and my loved ones' lives.
- **Loving.** To show my love for the people whom I love, in a concrete and regular way, at least once every day.
- **Committed.** To do what I say I am going to do, without emotional interference, humbly and calmly.
- **Cheerful.** To smile every morning, bring the smile to others around me.
- **Individual.** To find and work on my strengths, to accomplish my things suited to my abilities.
- **Accountable.** To take responsibility for my decisions even when things turn out badly.
- **Loyal.** Family is more important than work or colleagues.
- **Dignified.** To act in a manner that shows gentleness, humility, and politeness, as much as possible.
- **Boundaried:** To be clear on how much I can or give or receive to and from others, and to alter my behaviour appropriately depending on whom I am with.

Reflect on these things. Which ones resonate with you? What values would you add? What are your Rules of Engagement?

There is no pillow so soft as a clear conscience.

*The measure of a Muslim's character
is what he would do
if he knew no man could ever find out.*

*You can outrun things which chase you,
But not those things which run inside you.*

*Be as keen to seek freedom
As you are to avoid going where you are forbidden.*

*If you just focus on doing good,
the road ahead becomes a good one on its own.*

*Oh Allah,
Give us the courage not to give up what we think is right,
even when we think it is hopeless.*

Define your Rules of Conduct

Every Muslim aspires to Islamic principles. The Quran and Hadith are full of the finest examples of desirable behaviour, shown in allegories in the Quran, and the stories and sayings of the Prophet PBUH. Comb through them to enrich your heart with inspiration, noting down which rules particularly stand out for you. Why do they resonate for you particularly? Be confident in grasping them.

Other ways to concentrate on your Conduct:

1. Cast your mind forward in time. Imagine you're very old, looking back on your life. What character traits would you be proud of having shown throughout your life?

2. Advise your younger self. Imagine you were writing down a set of 10 rules that a child had to read, every morning and night. They had to act out those rules every day in order become a good and worthy person. What would those rules be?

3. Focus your list Now focus on the conduct rules that you are naturally really good at, and the ones you are weak at. Your Conduct rules should be in 3:1. For every 3 strengths-based rules, have one that focusses on an important weakness.

4. Repeat, Enrich, Apply.

Repetition is where you keep the list written close to you, and read it over frequently. In the morning, or evening, or after a meal. Have it on your phone, or as a voice recording.

Enrichment is when you read Quran and Hadith and contemplate its meaning, during Salah, or when you discuss and share your thoughts with someone else.

Application is when you face any event, joyous or sad, and look through your Rules to remember how to be.

Use this space for your own notes on the exercise opposite.

If you want to make an easy job seem much harder, keep putting it off.

We all procrastinate.

So, this is a bit uncomfortable. You are not alone in thinking you haven't done all the things you wanted to do. For some of us, if it wasn't for the last minute, we wouldn't get anything done.

The Quran says (18:23)
"And never say of anything, 'Indeed I will do it tomorrow'".

This is a warning against procrastination. Muslims are encouraged strongly not to procrastinate, and to be organised and moderate in our affairs. We have our days structured in school, which is why we felt we had such a busy time of it back then. Plan your day (Chapter 3).

It shouldn't surprise you that tackling procrastination is about lists and priorities. Life can become stressful when we have to keep thinking about what to do *next*. Never mind that- sometimes it can be difficult to pick out what needs done first. Left unattended, the issue gets worse, and then we find ourselves lurching from one emergency to another because we have lost control of our time.

The benefits of getting things done are measured in more than just achievement. There is a direct feeling of satisfaction that comes from attending to a task in hand. Doing something is its own reward, especially for people who struggle with living inside their own minds too much of the time. So much about mental health is addressed by distraction. Attendance to things on a list helps you to remain distracted in a productive way.

If you are overworked, or stressed, you can become overwhelmed. If you are clinically depressed or anxious, this is also the case. Depending on how bad the situation is, you might want to seek help. You can be busy or overworked but still be in a good mental place; this happens when you believe in what you do and it is providing a lot of good feedback to your sense of purpose and inner contentment.

Some people have naturally restless minds, struggling with knowing which things to do first, which to interrupt, and which to delegate or postpone.

The science

Be kind to yourself. Organising the mind is actually a more complex task than you might imagine. It is actually completed by a part of the brain that sits slightly outside the conscious parts. It is not in the Nafs, Intellect or Heart. It is within the connections between them, and it is called the *executive system.*

About 10% of people have problems with their executive system, and they end up chasing their tails, losing focus, getting distracted, or getting overly stuck into just one thing. This happens in the absence of anxiety or other issues. So these people find it very hard to stick to one thing, or they over-focus on one thing to the expense of everything else. They find it hard to coordinate their thoughts, and they may even have trouble creating and expressing language, or reading words as easily as others. These issues are sometimes seen in problems like autism, dyslexia, and attention deficit disorders, all of which are quite genetic in origin.

The positive side is that these people can often do certain things better than many others, like working with their hands, or being creative, or understanding computers. They are also very sympathetic and sensitive people by nature, because they have learned to understand what it is like to feel misunderstood. Society most offer these people both assistance for their problems, and special opportunities to develop their strengths. Alhamdulillah, they are part of the rich variety of humanity.

Instagram, March 2020

Getting things done

A task has to be something concrete, that you can actually do in the space of a day. So, start the day by writing out everything you want to get done. Just keep writing; empty your head. Make a long list.

Now, take the list and put items into each box below. Decide on whether it's urgent, important, or both. Put each onto the right box. Now, pick three in the 'do now' box, and get cracking.

Urgent and Important

DO NOW

Not Urgent, but Important

DO LATER

Urgent but not Important

DELEGATE/ OUTSOURCE

Not Urgent & Not Important

ELIMINATE

Time yourself: Whatever you do, take a 10 minute break hourly.

Use this space for your own notes on the exercise opposite.

Feeling Distant from Loved Ones

Life is all about relationships. Your relationship with yourself is a case in point. Are you kind to yourself? When you embark on something, do you accept your limitations and treat yourself in the same way you would with a very treasured guest or loved one? Or do you tell yourself off, blaming and finding fault? That is a relationship we have on the inside. It's better to treat yourself kindly: you spend a lot of time with yourself, and nobody likes a mean boss.

Beyond that, we have relationships with others. The Muslim is given rules and guidance as to how to approach these too. Look at the well-being box.

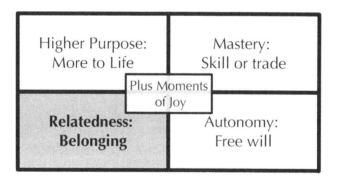

Relatedness, or belonging, is one of the keystones of the modern scientific view of well-being, and so it is with Islam. It is about the need for humans to feel a connection to others of their like. People have different ideas of who they prefer to be with, but it is fair to say that the first group that most people are part of is their family.

So how does the Muslim find wellbeing in family?

Through satisfying a deep-seated need in the Nafs: to belong. We live together, over and above differences in personality and values that inevitably exist between family members. This magic ingredient, if one were to give it a word, is love. It does not require a family member to like another, or even to get along with them. It just acts like a glue of acceptance which God tells the Muslim he should be very reluctant to ever let go of.

Allah tells the Muslim that the people are in his family are assigned to him, and he is assigned to them, and that they have a purpose in companionship, consultation, comfort, and assistance of each other which must be put above outside obligations.

This state of belonging provides for a number of advantages that are much greater than being in a non-related group. Mainly, the person has the space to feel loved unconditionally, and that he is eventually forgivable regardless of how badly he messes up. This does not happen in wider society, which is far less forgetful or forgiving.

For young married couples especially, it is difficult for your new husband or wife be the only person who supports you especially emotionally; you both would do far better by taking the pressure off each other. This is possible if you have close networks behind you on an everyday level- people who are around in the background, just being there for you. Overall, we are better off as part of a bigger network. Each

48

partner can feel supported by different people in the bigger family, in their locale, in their circle.

Connection to family has a price too, admittedly. Being part of a tribe involves compromises and sometimes keeping your mouth shut against your wishes. However, the payoff is that of maturity and integrity. It is through giving of ourselves that we discover strength and meaning to life.

It involves taking a risk. You might have to try really hard to do something that keeps the family happy, or pleases one particular person. You might get little back. Give of yourself, by giving your patience and unconditional acceptance of those you love, and inshallah you will receive the same back, but sometimes this might not happen.

If you don't get the bond you crave, you might be tempted to think that well, you tried, and break ties. But no.

The Prophet PBUH said *"The kinsman doesn't do it because he gets rewarded by his relatives in some way, but he persists in doing so even though they may have has severed ties with him"*

Does that seem like a tough job for you?

If so, consider this. A firm principle of psychological wellbeing is *tolerance and patience with the poor behaviour of others whom you value.*

The Hadith reminds us that our family bonds are always subject to waxing and waning, especially as we get older. Family members know each other far more deeply. This turns out to be one of the key advantages of family: they can accept our foibles and quirks, loving us and tolerating us regardless of what we are like. This is golden, precious jewel in the value of our family.

The Quran is quite clear on how much one's parents are to come above one's own concerns and opinions:
"And treat your parents with kindness. If they get old in your care, never be disgusted or answer back, but address them with respectful speech. Be humble to them out of mercy for them, and pray: 'My Lord! Be merciful to them for having cared for me in my childhood.'" (Quran 17:23-4)

So, if our parents become infirm, we are meant to be super-super nice to them. I look at this verse and see how much it seems to contrast a world where people are encouraged to speak their mind and not hesitate in challenging the authority of their parents when they see fit. Occasionally, we can and must disagree with our parents, gently and politely, if we feel very strongly about something, especially if there is a point of Islam or if they are being unfair to our spouse. But this should be the exception, not the rule.

How does the Muslim ever get to do his own thing? Is he obliged to go along with what the family wants?

This is a middle ground between the individual and the community. Cultures are often described as being either individual centric or community centric. Islam grants both things importance. To understand how this works, we look deeper and find that there are two main foundations, namely purpose and role.

The Muslim has **roles** in the family, which differ depending on which person he is dealing with. He could be brother, son, father, cousin and so on. Each of those roles demands specific attention and is examined as part of a Muslim's appraisal by God. If you imagine that every Muslim is being told this, then every Muslim should rightly feel that he is owed similar attentions by those who relate to him. It's a two way street: both give, and both receive.

The Muslim also has **purposes**, including fulfilling his religious duty, and to be of value to himself and others.

We could take work as a perfect example. The Muslim is encouraged to find work or knowledge which allows him to stand out and earn bread for his family. Women and men are permitted to do business and to learn skills, but to keep their family roles central.

Sadly, some countries limit or constrain women from finding work or education; a way that departs from Islamic truth. The cause may be to do with politics, or misinterpretation, or historical divisions and misguided cultural practices which still prevail depite Islamic guidance. Allah knows best, and may Allah help all of us to live more closely to His instructions. Ameen.

What about marriage and divorce? Does the Muslim face being shunned or punished if he is facing divorce?

Married couples who fall out are encouraged strongly to reconcile, but divorce is permitted. Some societies make divorce a total taboo, even forbidding it. Islam frowns on divorce, but permits it. Islam is realistic in its expectations of people in partnerships. People drift apart, and make unwise choices, or simply lose love for one another. This is the state of human beings, and Islam does not try to impose harsh irreversibility on marriage; after all it is one of the most fundamental sources of contentment and stability in life.

Islam is keen for people to get married; keener than other faiths. It is also keen for them to stay married and reconcile of they fall out, if possible. Evidence shows that for people who are even in unhappy marriages, persisting while there is still hope leads them to be happier than single people who have exited failed marriages.

And what about children who are adopted?

The adopted Muslim has as many rights and permissions as the biological one. The Prophet PBUH himself had an adopted son by the name of Zayd, whom he adopted after freeing from being a slave. It is therefore a great Sunnah (a desirable behaviour after prophetic tradition) to adopt and care for children if one has the inclination or opportunity to do so.

Comparing family with wider society

We are a social species. It is good to be independent, but we are even better when we are *inter*dependent on one another. Families are the first place where we learn how to be with other people. We learn social rules, cooperation, negotiation, and how to handle conflict and broken rules. Families are, in effect, mini-societies. Common rules, traditions, support structures, means of celebration and recreation, professions and labours, all come together in families.

In many current societies, nobody bats an eyelid when someone leaves their family ties to pursue a career or a partner. These freedoms are seductive for what they promise, offering independence and excitement, but these things come at a price. In departing from the family centre, we may lose this ready-made support without realising it at first.

Social isolation is significantly on the rise in most societies. Living alone is bad enough, but even living with just one's spouse is quite a stress. Young couples in particular have huge expectations from one another that are difficult to satisfy. Having family around takes the pressure off expecting the one spouse to be all the support.

Deferring decisions to the wider family is also quite freeing: it reduces the **cognitive load**. To explain what I mean, in closer families many decisions are grouped together. These are often everyday things such as buying provisions, how to celebrate special occasions, or even what assets to buy.

Giving up these things to the wider group is quite liberating; you are free to focus on what is more important to you, and you also get a greater prize: less stress, more loyalty and nurturance, and less expense too in the long run.

The family is also a way of ensuring that there are **economies of scale.** In a world where expenses are mounting, it makes more sense than ever for people to share where they live, share their labours in a joint business or profession, and share knowledge. This multiplies the wealth and comfort that the family as a whole enjoy. By all means, young people can go off to discover and learn, but returning to the family fold should be encouraged, never frowned nor insisted upon.

What does Islam have to say about friends?

Have a look at this picture:

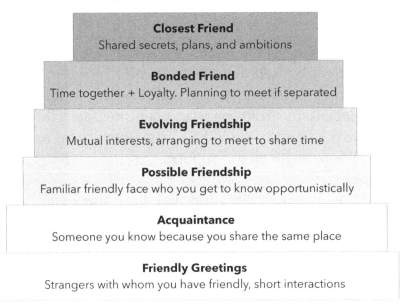

Closest Friend
Shared secrets, plans, and ambitions

Bonded Friend
Time together + Loyalty. Planning to meet if separated

Evolving Friendship
Mutual interests, arranging to meet to share time

Possible Friendship
Familiar friendly face who you get to know opportunistically

Acquaintance
Someone you know because you share the same place

Friendly Greetings
Strangers with whom you have friendly, short interactions

54

The Muslim is encouraged to have friends, and Islam takes a rather refined approach to friendship. Friends are not romanticised as being automatically the natural deepest companions of anyone. There are grades of frienship, and different boundaries and expectations of different types of friends and family.

First off, the Muslim is advised to judge and choose his friends with some discretion. He is advised to associate with people of high character. He is also advised to be careful about how much he chooses to invest in a friend.

For example, sharing secrets and confidential things is not desirable early on. People make the mistake of disclosing too much in an effort to claim or gain friendship, but doing so puts both them and the other person at risk: expectations are set too high. If the friendship fails or doesn't have enough time served, the secret could be leaked out and cause harm.

There are many Hadith and Quranic verses advising on what emerges as a studied and highly tuned approach to friendship. This does not mean at all that one must be hesitant from having friends or be ready to shut them out at the slightest transgression. Rather, it means that we are to regard friends with warmth, and be on the lookout for opportunities to make friends who remind us of the best character traits we aspire to. Psychologically, this is sound: characters tend to form similarly in similar company.

Finally, the Muslim is advised that the truest of friends is judged not by the ones who we have good times with, but the ones who are there for us even when we are absent, ill, facing disaster or death. Again, this is a sound psychological basis of character.

Not for the Muslim is the meek and very vulnerable approach of seeing everyone as a potential friend who should be given every trust. The Muslim is encouraged to be friendly with all, but be very clear about who he lets into his actual confidence. This is a startlingly realistic point of view, founded on a sound principle.

We are all given to different levels of loyalty and different types of behaviour depending on who we are with. People in general can seem very friendly or sincere on the surface, but this is part of a social norm. We are advised that a temporary interaction with them in a professional or other context is not to be taken as an indication of their emotional outlook, nor of what their true beliefs are, when it comes to the crunch.

Muslims as a worldwide group

Something magical happens in Islam. Muslims are much more emotionally united than other faiths. Look at how the Muslim, on hearing news that another Muslim in some far off country has suffered harm, gets very upset, far more than one would expect for someone who is essentially a stranger. There is something very deeply tethering and rooted about just being a Muslim in the world. It is a community which feels its pain and shares its joys more acutely than most. Feel that brotherhood. **Volunteering** for your Ummah improves both your wellbeing and helps other Muslims. A double win.

Get closer to your family

Families relate more deeply with their emotions and egos than just with cold logic or intellect. Expect this:

Just talking. It's more important than what is talked about.
Hierarchy. Seniors like to be respected and deferred to.
Collectivism. Sharing each other's things is preferred.
Rallying. Supporting someone regardless of what they did.
Gatherings. Easier than ever, now with virtual video.

 Pick any of the following, and try it:

1. **Give gifts** frequently. A sunnah of the prophet PBUH, who exchanged sweets, perfumes, honey and the like.

2. **Think.** 'What little thing can I do to make X happy today?' Smallest acts of thoughtfulness bring love.

3. **Contact.** A regular phone call. That Sunday night chat with loved ones is treasured and often surprisingly helpful.

4. **Understand** about your family history. What was life like for your them in the old days? Where do we come from? It builds strength, respect and a strong bonded culture to learn about your family history as much as you can.

5. **Ask** for advice and help. Sharing a problem creates unity. It gives a sense of inter-dependency: the lifeblood of family.

Use this space for your own notes on the exercise opposite.

**A bend in the road is never the end of the road.
You just have to make a turn.**

When Difficulties Seem Overwhelming

When a Muslim experiences a difficulty, he is gleeful in anticipation. A Muslim has been commanded to understand difficulties as both a chance and a test. He therefore sees opportunity.

The **chance** part is about how we can solve a difficult problem. Facing difficulties is an opportunity for us to gain respect for ourselves.

The **test** part is about how we show our true character. In other words, what exists in our Hearts. The Quran tells Muslims quite specifically that they are judged by what they have in their Hearts, sometimes with stern vigour:

And most certainly have We destined for hell many of the invisible beings and men who have hearts with which they fail to grasp the truth.

As scary as it sounds, this verse isn't at all that scary for the Muslim, because he's already on the right side of it. Muslims believe that truth is easy to accept, and our character is focussed on accepting the facts and difficulties of life exactly as we find them. It makes life a lot less complicated. It's easy to smile when you know that your character is centred around truth, not opinion.

As a doctor of the mind, I can attest that coping and overcoming difficulties provide greater long term rewards and satisfactions in people than short term, easy wins. Study after study proves this. That said, it is not all struggle and work. You do need to find simple things in your day that allow you to feel instant joy- happiness has both short term and long term ingredients.

In scientific terms, difficulty challenges us to use our Intellect, and to discipline our emotions (Nafs). This takes a good deal of effort, but when the two components work together we a sense of satisfaction that is long-lived.

A simple diagram of the Muslim Mind

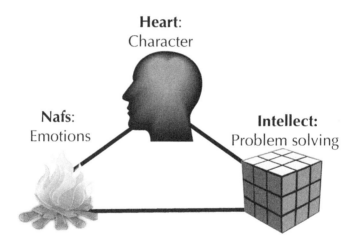

When you approach a complex problem, the three parts of your mind often see things differently.

The Nafs reacts first, with its emotions and instincts. *What is this issue? It looks very easy/ very hard! No problem, leave it til later! Do it right away or you will look like a loser!* Anything with a strong emotional signal, and usually over-reactive.

The Intellect looks for facts and truths, and tries to understand the issue logically. *Who, what, why, where, when? What do I know about this matter? Can other people assist? What kind of priority does this actually have?*

The Heart sees things in context: *What are the Nafs and Intellect saying? How does this issue fit with my wish to be a good person? How could I solve the problem in a way that would please Allah and the people affected by it?*

This is a very powerful system once you understand how it operates. You have three ways of looking at something. Ideally, the most integrated way is that of the Heart: your true judge, your True self. It takes into account the fullness of your being, and in so doing helps you to make a wise decision in the end.

So we have two elements of happiness: short term and long term. Short term ones are moments of joy that come from simple acts of remembrance, kindness, savouring everyday things like a kindly smile, beauty in nature, and so on.

Long term happiness is from approaching challenge. We can plan to do something difficult but worthwhile, such as study for a career or organise something in the community, or a difficulty can visit us, such as an accident, a change in circumstances and such like. It matters not: we see both things as part of our strategy to enrich our lives with a noble, cheerful struggle to find long term contentment.

Approach a difficulty as a challenge

Every difficulty is an opportunity to find a solution, either to avoid it, cope with it, solve it.

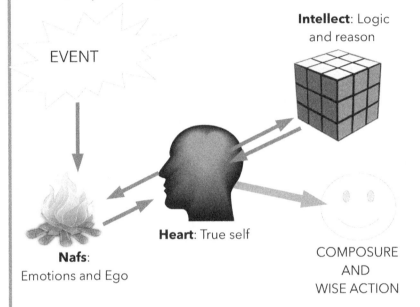

Intellect: Logic and reason

EVENT

Heart: True self

Nafs: Emotions and Ego

COMPOSURE AND WISE ACTION

Next time you face a difficulty, know this:

1. The emotions will react first. They are strong, and very tempting to act on. Relax. Don't act on them. Wait. Breathe.
2. Use your intellect. It searches for TRUTHS and FACTS, and applies logic and reason.
3. Listen to all parts of your mind. Generate a long list of solutions, from simple through to silly. It doesn't matter, just keep going until you have at least twenty of them.
4. Congratulations. Now pick which one appeals to your Heart, and go with it. Say Bismillah!

Use this space for your own notes on the exercise opposite.

Prayer does not change Allah,
but praying to Allah does change the one who prays.

Feeling Unheard with Nobody To Talk To

A Muslim has certain daily obligations. One of those is prayer. If we look at the reason for why prayers are compulsory, we learn that God has made those things mandatory which are most beloved of him.

In other words, God is extremely fond of when the Muslim takes the chance to communicate with him, so much so that it is compulsory to do so. Those five prayers are times when the Muslim gets to completely exclude the outside world and have only God in their focus.

Checking in like this, detaching from the demands of the material world and going to a spiritual place, is one of the key pieces of advice that both Islam and science encourage. This can be both physical and mental.

For the physical part, we know what to do. The movement parts of salah (standing, kneeling, prostrating etc) are part of *kinaesthetic* learning: the movements themselves help train the mind and settle it towards achieving focus.

The mental part is often overlooked; we go through the motions of salah mechanically. This is a missed opportunity to become among **those who reflect.** The Quran repeatedly refers to those who reflect as being more blessed and closer to Allah. Salah is an audience with Allah! We have an open line to actually talk to God. Salah gives is multiple daily opportunities to communicate with Him; it is the ideal chance for reflection and discovery.

We are advised to speak to Allah both in and out of salah. When praying to God asking or confessing anything, the Muslim is instructed to do so with a certain optimism and verve, in a way, to pray as if what he/she is asking for will definitely be heard, and Allah will answer by either giving it, delaying it, or providing some alternative reward which is better for the person. But we must ask!

Asking for something from God is not so much hopeless begging; it is better to be done in a spritely and positive way.

Confessing something to God is not to be done with a sense of hopelessness. Remorse must be felt with a mixture of repentance and positive determination: a positive and hopeful resolution not to repeat the bad deed.

If one is overwhelmed by life and feels like crying, then doing so to God is equally encouraged. You do not need human company if you cannot find it. Allah himself will gladly hear you out and receive your pain unconditionally.

If we can't find the words, Allah doesn't even need for us to open our mouths. If the need is too painful, or somehow cannot find words, God hears it from us anyway. It pays huge dividends to confess that you are at your limit with something, that you might be struggling with patience, restraint or other people. Do you think Allah will ignore you? Never. So confirm that you are not ignoring Him!

God knows the human condition only too well: nothing you can say will surprise Him, and nothing you can tell him is beyond his help. Making du'aa is scientifically useful too: it allows the different parts of the mind, conflicted with facts and emotions and memories, to reach a steady state of acceptance. It does so because evidence suggests that prayer, confession and reflection require active efforts to connect parts of ourselves that are in conflict; the brain is quieter and calmer as a result.

The belief of Tawheed- the Oneness of Allah- has embedded in it the idea that He is everywhere, and runs all affairs. Muslims are encouraged to rely on Allah. Psychologically, this is a practical enactment of one of the highest principles of human wellbeing: acceptance that there is much more meaning to life than just the everyday. We reclaim our sense of perspective on things, unsticking the mind from places where it gets bogged down.

Instagram, March 2020

Making du'aa with enthusiasm

The strongest general Hadith about du'aa is this one:
"When any one of you prays, let him start by praising Allah, then let him send blessings upon the Prophet, then let him say du'aa' however he wishes." [Tirmidhi]. For notes on the etiquette of formal du'aas, consult your own Madhab.

For du'aas that you make on your own, remember these things:

1. **You can ask God for help at any time.** You can say it in your mind. You need not be anywhere special.

2. **Ask for things while you are in salah itself.** You have established the contact with Allah, and are already in communion with him. Ask for whatever you need to.

3. **There is no time you can't ask.** All you need to do is silently speak to God; you need not even be in a clean state.

4. **You can say anything you feel** you need to say to your Maker; you can confess things you dare not confess out loud to anyone else. Let it out. It will feel so much better.

5. **Ask with conviction and optimism.** He loves to hear our prayers, but even more so when we say them with true belief, courage and optimism.

Voicing your problems out loud to Allah on your own, is in itself directly helpful to the brain. You are taking the problem and constructing it into words, and literally listening to yourself. Answers seem to arise on their own. Allah answers your prayer often within the moments you are making the prayer itself! Alhamdulillah!

Use this space for your own notes on the exercise opposite.

**Ignore excessive criticism, and welcome true praise.
Both things come from within you.
Learn to be a friend to yourself.**

If we Overlook our Strengths, or Focus on our Faults.

Do you believe that God is fair?

Why yes, of course I do.

Well, He's much more than that. He's actually biased in our favour. Let me explain. He forgives far more than he punishes. This gives us great confidence to embrace our lives with courage, and to focus on our strengths.

Muslims believe that their imperfections are part of their intentional design by the Almighty. The Muslim is aware that despite his best efforts, he will fail, make bad judgments and decisions. He is aware that he will be inadequate in the amount he repents, keep his resolutions, or resists nefarious temptations. This would seem to stack the odds against him, but it doesn't. God's forgiveness balances it out.

Muslims have been told by God that He is far readier to forgive them for their misdeeds than to punish them. And as for their good deeds, their God prefers to multiply their blessings and his pleasures at witnessing these.

Subhanallah! Allah is fully acquainted with the man's tendency to make bad decisions, letting him off the hook for doing so as long as he repents sincerely. He wants to make life, and the afterlife, easy for us.

It makes for a far more settled state of mind, and actually makes us less likely to sin, if we know that our Maker has such deep love for us. He is ready to turn a blind eye to our gravest errors if we just ask him for forgiveness and resolve not to repeat them.

This inspires confidence. Life is full of trials, errors, and temptations, and moments when we lose our judgment. The conscientious Muslim sleeps far more easily knowing that he can act with optimism. He can go firmly in life knowing that he might make an unforeseen error, but that Allah is ready to forgive. If there is something that brings out a human being's finest behaviour more than anything else, it is the feeling of being **believed in**. His forgiveness is clear evidence of how much Allah believes in us and wants us to go out there and live fully.

Doesn't that make a person more likely to sin? Like they have a 'get out of jail free' card?

Only a person of weak character behaves in a way that is more sinful because of the freedom they have. For the rest of us, we actually thrive with it. We don't abuse our freedom because God knows if our intentions are to do good.

God tells Muslims that he will never punish them for their bad intentions, but He will readily reward them for having good intentions even before they act on them. The Muslim feels nurtured, understood and loved by God in a deeply comforting way. What a marvellous feeling that must be.

Science reinforces how this works psychologically. 'Unconditional positive regard' and strengths-based development, also known by other acronyms such as RAID (Reward the Appropriate, Ignore the Destructive), are proven to be very effective techniques in modifying adults' behaviour towards the positive. These approaches are perfect mimics of the original and greatest, wonderfully merciful rose-tinted way in which God himself prefers to look at his creations.

In therapy sessions and professional coaching, professionals are aware of the magic 3 to 1 ratio of strength-to-deficiency discussions. To explain, in working with anyone who wants to improve their behaviour or thinking in some way, it is most effective to spend 75-80% of the time talking about their strengths and virtues, and the remaining 25-30% of the time discussing their weaknesses or failures.

It is as if enlarging the positive elements has an energising effect on the fragile soul of a person, thereby giving him the energy and confidence to tackle his weaker parts more optimistically. This energy is built up best when we spend most of the time focussing on our strengths.

Mind Training Session: Finding Your strengths

Find and grow the talents that you were given.

Types of strength:

Heart: Deen, Wisdom, Morality, Judgment, Conduct, Resilience, Stability, Self awareness, Listening, Humour

Intellect: Knowledge, Logic, Planning, Focus, Curiosity, Cooperation, Rule-following, Analytical ability, Reliability

Nafs/Emotion: Sociability, Emotional awareness, Intuition, Playfulness, Creativity, Loyalty, Energy, Comforting, Physical

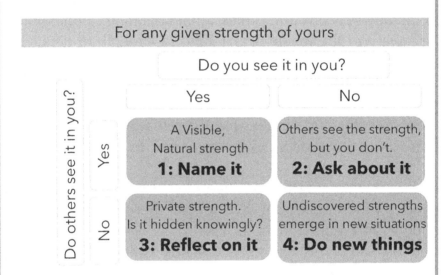

For any given strength of yours

Do you see it in you?

	Yes	No
Do others see it in you? — Yes	A Visible, Natural strength **1: Name it**	Others see the strength, but you don't. **2: Ask about it**
Do others see it in you? — No	Private strength. Is it hidden knowingly? **3: Reflect on it**	Undiscovered strengths emerge in new situations **4: Do new things**

For each area of the mind: Heart, Intellect and Nafs:

Do the following, referring to the numbered squares:

1. Celebrate it! Name the strength. It's yours, in the bank.

2. Get feedback! Ask others their opinion on your strengths

3. Reflect on it. How could you make it more visible?

4. Do new things! It's the way to find hidden strengths.

Your prize is better knowledge of your strengths.

Use this space for your own notes on the exercise opposite.

A person abandons control over life
by depending too much on what others think.

Not Feeling in Control

Muslims believe that although God knows our destinies, He has given us the free will to act as we choose. We have the responsibility of being in control of how to react to things, and how to steer our lives. Let's look again at the box of wellbeing:

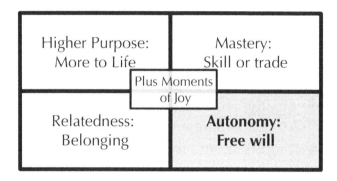

So, psychologically it is very important for people to have autonomy: a sense of freedom and independence of thoughts and actions. This means taking responsibility for everything that happens, whether it's your fault or not. It doesn't mean you become responsible for a lightning bolt or earthquake, but it does mean you are responsible for looking out for these hazards and dealing with them properly if and when they happen. And bad things happen.

How does responsibility actually improve the Muslim's contentment?

Through giving them control. Giving them accountability. To be responsible for one's actions seems like a burden, but it's actually the opposite.

Think about it this way. God has given you the freedom to act as you see fit. You get to put in whatever effort you like, into whatever you choose. You can also react to anything in the way you like.

What does this allow you to do? Well, you get to look at your decisions and change them if they didn't work out. You get free reign to face challenges and problems in your life and become creative and optimistic in addressing them. You can, if you like, try to change the whole world for the better. What an enormous blessing this responsibility actually is!

But what if you fail, or if terrible things happen outside your control?

Allah controls your destiny: you just control yourself. Being responsible for what happen for your life does not mean that you literally control your destiny. The Muslim knows that the job is simply to do their best with what they have have in front of them. The results, and unexpected changes, are beyond the Muslim's control. For this part, the Muslim relies on Allah. And whatever happens, good or bad, guess what?

...Allah has put something useful in it for the person?
Yup, now you're starting to get it.

Islam was a liberating force for many peoples when it first arrived. Rights and freedoms were given to women, slaves, prisoners and even animals, in a way that had never quite been accepted up to that point.

If you stop a person from acting of their own free will without good reason, whether husband, wife, father or stranger, you face a grave consequence from Allah because you have taken away what He has given to that person.

Whatever happens in your life, if it affects you, it is your responsibility to face it properly. If you made a bad decision, you take responsibility for it. If you took bad advice, it was still your decision to take that advice. Take responsibility. The more you do it, the more accurately you can work out where you can change for the better.

But life can hit you hard. Won't Muslims try less hard if they know that they are free to act but can't control the result?

You are right, life does hit very hard. When you realise that Allah is control of the result, you gain a sense of happiness because you can let go of that part. You begin to apply your efforts in a wiser, more measured way, combining gentleness with intelligence and persistence. It is a far less exhausting way to live. Not anger, over-reaction or complaining about things being unfair.

True strength is gentle, and true gentleness is strong. The wise doctor says that he provides the treatment, but God provides the cure.

Being controlled by other's opinions

It is unwise to worry too much about what other people think of us. People will like us or dislike us regardless of what we do. God tells the Muslim that popularity and fame are a not a measure of a Muslim's character. It's to do with what psychologists call the 'locus of control'. You can be the driver or the passenger in your life; it is better to be the driver most of the time, to have *internal* locus of control.

To be liked by many people does not indicate that a person has a good Heart. It could just mean that they have managed to appeal to someone for the wrong reasons. Those who become popular for the right reasons, for example their compassion, generosity or learnedness, may also fall into the trap of seeking popularity or recognition for their deeds. This is also discouraged.

As an example, the Quran says
" Do not cancel your charity by reminding people of your generosity or by injury, like those who spend their wealth in order to be noticed by people..." (2:264)

But isn't it good to become well known if you do great things?

Sure, but becoming well known is not something you should seek. If you become well known, it is a side effect of the quality of your character, your work and by your humble efforts, not by seeking the fame for its' own sake.

What's the difference? Can't a person try to get famous if he is trying to do good work, to spread his influence?

This makes sense on the surface, but there is deep wisdom as to why it doesn't work. What happens is that you become distracted by the popularity and fame itself, forgetting the real reasons and purposes of what you are doing.

Does that mean you can't promote yourself? What if you are trying to win an election or promote a charity?

Well, that's a complex but interesting point, and we can tackle it all the same. Let's suppose you are a politician with very sound ideas, but you need to win an election to get power. The correct way, in ideal circumstances, would be to promote your stand on your principles and qualities, and people decide on their own. If you try to change your principles for people because you need their vote, you will lose yourself.

But shouldn't you be responsive to what people want and need?

There's a difference between what people want and what they need. In the real world, it's common for politicians to promise people what they want just to get elected. Usually some kind of fantasy of free money, a crimeless nation, or better hospitals and so on. Often, they don't deliver. You may have to attract people's interest by appealing to their Nafs-their base desires, often unrealistic and irrational.

If your actual intentions are genuine and good, then you might decide that a degree of exaggeration is a worthy means to an end. God knows what you are intending at all times. But if you win, you better not be doing anything immoral or deceptive when you actually get power, because that is what you will be judged on by God himself.

The Muslim is warned about the dangers and temptations that come with being controlled by what others think of you. It is too much of a burden on the ego- the Nafs- to resist the constant temptation to be liked. It leaves a person very unsteady on their feet. Needing constant validation from other people doesn't make for a steady emotional mind.

It's more common now than ever for people, especially younger folk, to measure their worth by how many people show interest in what they say or do. Social media are a minefield for this. It will be a tough road for many young folk, many of whom have not developed their Intellects and Hearts enough to see these forces for what they really are.

Likewise, the Muslim is deeply discouraged from spreading or being involved in rumours or gossip about others. It is understandable why rumours happen. People like to know what is going on, and when facts aren't clear, people use their intuition to guess. They may be right or wrong, but the damage that comes from wrong guesses is huge.

Unfortunately, many a good person's life has been torn down because of rumour. This is why a Muslim has no part in it. He ought to be aware of rumours, and put them right if he feels if he feels he has the credibility to do so. Otherwise, he is encouraged to distance himself from the rumour-spreaders.

Instagram, March 2020

Reclaim your Locus of Control

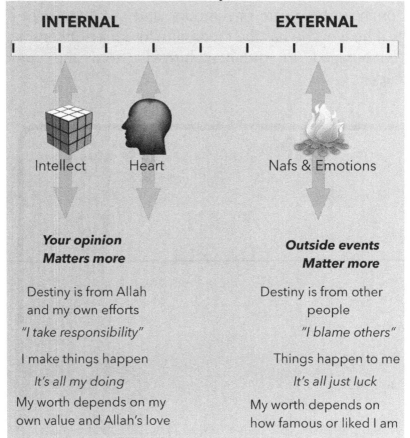

Where does the control of your life come from?

INTERNAL	EXTERNAL
Intellect Heart	Nafs & Emotions
Your opinion Matters more	**Outside events Matter more**
Destiny is from Allah and my own efforts	Destiny is from other people
"I take responsibility"	*"I blame others"*
I make things happen	Things happen to me
It's all my doing	*It's all just luck*
My worth depends on my own value and Allah's love	My worth depends on how famous or liked I am

Think through your own instinctive reactions about how your life is. Are you the driver or the passenger? The wise person knows that he is mostly to be the driver, but to have some sympathy and awareness for what the outside world thinks.

Look where the Heart is. 75%+ of your emotions are yours to own and account for. Only allow maximum 25% to be externally determined. More than 25%, you lose your emotional stability and you will find it difficult to take responsibility for your actions.

Use this space for your own notes on the exercise opposite.

What happiness and joy can be found around you!
The sooner you realise that, the happier you will be.

Not enough happy moments.

This chapter is about how the truly happy person frequently reports feelings of joy and wonder at the world around them, simply on a sensory level. It is also about the joy or pleasure you get when appreciating your position as part of Allah's vast and unknown creation, and when you see yourself or someone you love doing a good thing, no matter how small or big.

In the Wellbeing Box, moments of joy can and should be allowed to pop up throughout our daily lives.

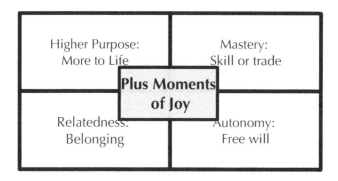

How is it that the arrangement of bones and skin of a face could render someone more attractive than another? Why does a sweet scent soften the temper and ease a conversation? How could such a thing be fair? Why is it that we inherently love such curious things as the stars in the sky? Why are we moved by beauty to make decisions which we would normally cause us to hesitate?

In the Quran, God tells Muslims:

"Attractive to man is the enjoyment of worldly desires through women, and children, and heaped-up treasures of gold and silver, and horses of high mark, and cattle, and lands. All this may be enjoyed in the life of this world, but the most beauteous of all goals is with God."

Quran 3:14

Because of statements like these, Muslims feel no guilt or shame in appreciating beauty or the pleasures of the senses responsibly, within the rules. The prophet PBUH was known to love sweet foods, to wear pleasant fragrances, and to wear fine or new clothing especially on auspicious days. He was keen on being properly groomed. Muslims know to follow this example. If our appearance and demeanour pleases another, we earn Allah's pleasure. When we appreciate the joy that another brings, we praise them and Allah for that moment.

The way in which beauty or other pleasantries can soothe the soul of the beholder is not viewed as unfair or deceptive, unless it is used for a devious act. Rather, the person who has beauty or charm is notified by God that these assets can be taken away at any time, and that having them involves handling them responsibly.

If one feels without physical beauty then there is benefit and responsibility that comes with that too. For each person, whatever they sense, enjoy and possess are all things for which an account is made and to be reckoned with.

God tells the Muslim that everything is going to be called to account. How did you deal with your beauty? How much did your pleasures distract you? The glorious things in the world that we can taste, see, hear, feel and touch, are all to be taken as rightly enjoyable, and kept fresh by having them sporadically, not indulging ourselves in them all the time. They are temporary comforts alone. God will judge what is in our Hearts.

Nature itself is full of delights for Man, being filled with immense scale, strength, fragility, tenderness and sheer incomprehensible facts and mysteries. Again, the Muslim is told that these are the signs of God's mercy and power. A Muslim is told to appreciate and contemplate these things as surely and regularly as he would do everyday things like drinking water or putting on fine clothing.

All of these things exist in a way to excite, stimulate and energise the emotions and soul of a person- his *Nafs* and *Ruh*. Mankind is not to avoid these things, because there is goodness and refreshment within them. The sight of the jagged peak of Mount Everest, piercing a deep blue sky with a trail of freezing mist caressing the very tips of the rocks is enough to bring about some sense of connection with the Divine, the cosmic, the insignificance of our being.

The Muslim does not shy away from these feelings, discarding them as wistful poetic distraction. No- the Muslim is encouraged to invest his time and his mind in using these experiences to enrich his life, to teach and inspire others, and to remember the favours that God has given to him.

91

Were we all to live without these pleasures, it would be doubtful that we would ever achieve great things either individually or as a species. People need to be invigorated, inspired, provoked and ignited into action and reaction very often, to give them spark and momentum.

Scientifically, there is again very sound basis to this. It turns out that well-being and contentment with life are related to the frequency and regularity of good sensory and emotional moments: a life where the ability to enjoy ones' senses is both frequent and desirable. Savour life, all parts of it.

Not for the Muslim is the pain of the ascetic, the denial of the Catholic, or the detachment of the Buddhist. The Muslim draws from the benefit of positive experiences. In prayer, and in meditation, the Muslim gets to reset his physical and emotional self to appreciate these things all over again.

In Ramadan, the Muslim invests further into this philosophy by restricting his pleasures in a strict timetable. This is known very obviously to have significant benefits for the physical health, but what is emerging into the evidence is the emotional and spiritual revival that the month brings. Practising self-denial is one of the surest ways of learning to gain respect for oneself.

There are limits and conditions to what pleasures and indulgences are allowable, set by God for the Muslim. Whilst this might seem like a suffocating space for those who believe that Muslims are repressed or robotic, in reality these limitations are a sanctuary for the soul.

Limitations, it turns out, are exactly what is required for true freedom to be experienced. It looks counter-intuitive but in nature, there is no respect for counter-intuition: things just are as they are. Too much indulgence in any sensory pleasure dulls the joy of it.

Excessive immersion into addictive joys is corrupting to the personality and destructive to one's sense of command of one's own actions. Your Nafs gets out of control and you get stuck as an addict.

For all the pleasures that are promised and provided, the Muslim is also grateful that his God has given them a 'dos and don'ts' guide as to how to appreciate them constructively and responsibly. Alhamdulillah for such comprehensive instructions!

There is one more curious thing about moments of joy: they are enjoyed that much more when they are shared, or given to, other people. To give joy to others is equally potent in bringing joy to one self, as well as earning great pleasure from Allah.

<u>Appreciate Moments of Joy</u>

1. Spend a few minutes on each of these things, giving thanks to Allah for what He has created in an instant of will.

Beauty: There is beauty near you could be in a pattern on some fabric, in a tree nearby. Find it. Inspect and appreciate it. Darwin's Orchid (left) shows delicacy and hardiness combined. It hangs on to life dependent on a single creature.

Complexity: This moth the only thing that can fertilise Darwin's Orchid. It needs to have a proboscis (tongue) 4 times the length of its body, to get the nectar. The moth and the flower can live *only* from each other.

Awe: Look up into the night. Among billions of planets, one *55 Cancri*, is 8 times the size of Earth, and made almost completely of solid diamond. Contemplate the vast Universe.

Power: This is Mount Everest. You probably don't know that it used to be underwater. It was lifted out of the sea by colliding it with the Asian continent. An easy thing for God.

2. Go out in nature. At least once a week. Concentrate on the sights, sounds, scents, **everything** you perceive. This is proven to help well-being in very significant amounts. A walk, or a hike, can and does improve wellbeing. We know this scientifically and spiritually. Enjoy your time in nature slowly, gently, taking time to savour everything from your senses. People who spend time in nature are more healthy and less stressed: this is a proven fact.

Use this space for your own notes on the exercise opposite.

Sketch, in a very simple way, something you see.

Eat something small but delicious, slowly and carefully. Describe in detail what it looks, like. What effect does it have on you before you eat it?

Describe a favourite thing of yours to look at. A car, a mountain, anything. What makes is beautiful to you?

Feel wonder at something Allah has created.
Say Alhamdulillah.

This is Cancri 55. A planet.

8 times the size of Earth.
Made almost completely of
solid diamond.

Instagram, March 2020

Losing One's Smile.

As Muslims, we are followers of the prophet Muhammad (Peace Be Upon Him). His Hadith are the words and records that were made of him during and in the years after his passing. They are extensive. Islamic scholars estimate around 10 thousand authentic (as in more reliable) Hadith.

The prophet PBUH smiled. A lot. Abdullah ibn al-Harith reported:

"I have not seen anyone smile more often than the Messenger of Allah, peace and blessings be upon him."
-al-Tirmidhī Hadith

We are meant to model our behaviour on that of our beloved Prophet PBUH. It's as simple as that. Mufti Menk gives us a clue as to why smiling is such a useful thing:

"Smiles are amazing. They hide so much: pain, fear, sadness...but they reflect strength. A smile is one of the best acts of charity."

Clearly, one who smiles has got reasons to be smiling. We are unafraid of anything that life brings to us. We walk with the assumption that everything that happens, good or bad, is fixed within our destiny, long before our birth. As we go through life we discover our destiny unfolding before us. We were created by our Allah himself, who loves us deeply. What a privilege to be alive! That is reason enough to smile.

Appreciate this, because if you do, then you might start to believe a higher truth. We are all born into our life story. How we choose to write our own story depends on what attitude we choose to adopt. If you still have enough reserve in you to smile more, and find reasons and excuses to smile at others, then start today. A smile is one of the easiest and quickest victories that we can possibly achieve.

Even smiling in the face of pain and difficulty is useful. Studies show, surprisingly, that even when you do this, the brain finds reasons to believe you might be happy. People find they feel happier after smiling on their own for a few minutes.

Simple Smiling Exercises: Mind Training Box

Why learn about smiling? *There is no shame in trying to learn how to carry out the Sunnah in an effective way!*

1. **Practice**. A true smile is all over your face. It is especially seen in the eyes. Spend some time checking your smile in the mirror. As odd as that seems, you will get to learn a little bit about what is convincing. Actors and public figures get lessons on smiling for this very reason.

2. **Try smiling at someone** in a friendly way. Watch them. Most of them can't help but smile back. Be glad; you have just made someone happier, for a few seconds.

3. **When you are speaking to someone**, try smiling. Evidence shows that they will like you more, and the tone of your voice changes. People who were asked to listen to just voices on the phone, were able to tell which people were smiling. They rated those voices as more pleasant and convincing.

4. **Try even when you don't feel like it.** Studies show, surprisingly, that even when you do this, the brain finds reasons to believe you might be happy. People find they feel happier after smiling on their own for a few minutes.

5. **Laugh.** Find a reason to laugh, every day, at yourself, or something amusing. It lowers blood pressure and improves stress management too.

Use this space for your own notes on the exercise opposite.

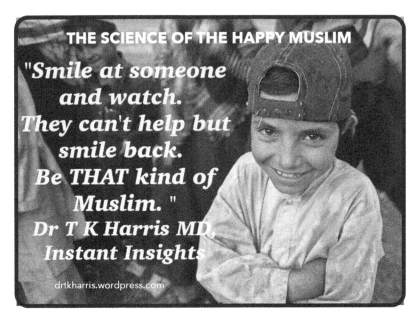

Instagram, March 2020

Missing the deep meaning of 'Muslim'

The Arabic word salaam ("peace") originates from the same root as the word Islam: *peace,* and *submission*. The Islamic outlook is that individual personal peace is attained by utterly submitting to Allah.

In the ideal world, it's hard to imagine why anyone who calls themselves peaceful would be otherwise. We do live in the real world though, so it's not a surprise that Muslims, and every other religion for that matter, have got caught up in some un-peaceful things.

Individual peace doesn't always translate into peace in the external world. In fact, true personal peace exists in spite of the noise and mayhem of the world outside the body. The Muslim accepts that no matter how much peace he might find in himself, he will not be able to change the parts of the world outside his control.

Fine, but what concrete things can you actually do to become inwardly peaceful?

You are asking the right questions now. Trying to see how to live like the definition of a Muslim. The root of a wise life is not just in saying something, but actually doing stuff to live by those values. If your mind is a noisy and unsettled place, and you want to become more like those very calm, serene kind of people who seem unruffled by life, then you need to do things to settle it.

Consider the makeup of the Muslim's mind again:

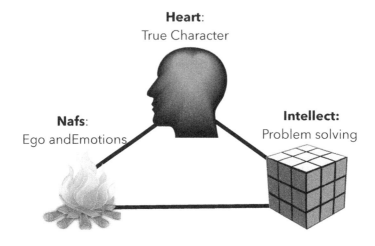

Heart:
True Character

Nafs:
Ego andEmotions

Intellect:
Problem solving

Each one of those parts is busy trying to appraise the world around you, so you see things in different angles, often conflicting ones. You scramble around trying to make sense of it, but this just makes you feel more confused.

The sensible thing to do would be to become more accepting of this state of being. Once this happens, you can see things more clearly. Anxiety diminishes and you can take situations in your stride. Salah is one of the most powerful ways of separating yourself from the noise. It is your time to commune with Allah alone. This is the first and original way of calm.

Another way is by meditation. So let's get to it. Training page on Islamic meditation next.

The prophet PBUH received many of the revelations of the Quran while meditating in the Cave of Hira

Islamic meditation

The prophet PBUH spent many days and nights, over many years, in meditation. There are different ways in which you can meditate. To do so formally, you could find a shaykh who would help guide you through it. However, here is a simple method to try on your own. Frequency:10-20 minutes daily

Choose a quiet place to sit, away from distractions.

Sit on the floor or on a chair, whatever is comfortable, with your back straight.

Stare ahead on a fixed point in the middle distance, looking slightly beyond it, or close your eyes.

Take slow, deep breaths in and out. Use your full chest.

Concentrate on your breathing. Focus purely on this, as much as you can. Take time to enjoy getting it right.

Repeat the process for a total of ten full breath cycles.

Imagine the word 'Allah' slowly sounding at the pace of your heart beating. It might help if you want to say it out loud, softly, just under your breath.

Invite your attention back to your breathing if you intrusion from distractions. It's Ok to feel distracted. Accept it, and return to your inner rhythmic voice of *Allah.. Allah..Allah*.

The Nafs will become quieter and more still, the more you do this.

Let your mind wander if it wants to, but whatever you are feeling, whatever you are thinking, do not question its content.

Be thankful to Allah for the opportunity to experience your mind and body in this way.

End the process at any time; just count down from 10 breaths to zero. That's it!

Use this space for your own notes on the exercise opposite.

**Worry and action don't go together easily.
You can't wring your hands and roll your sleeves up
at the same time.**

Lost in Worry about the Past or the Future

The contented Muslim is unconcerned with worries of the past and future. The Prophet PBUH said:

"When evening comes, do not expect (to live till) morning, and when morning comes, do not expect (to live till) evening. Take from your health (a preparation) for your illness, and from your life for your death."

But doesn't that mean you will never learn from the past? Or you might miss something bad coming in the future?

Living in the present moment does not mean that you fail to reflect on the past, or that you don't plan for the future.

Reflecting on the past, and planning and anticipating things for the future, are business of a sound Intellect and a good Heart. However, worrying about things you cannot change, be they past or future, is not. That is more the work of the Nafs, tempted as it is to ruminate, regret, fear and worry.

There is a line between reflection and rumination. That line is defined by mood and outlook. Looking back on mistakes happily with a sense of optimism and a wish to learn a lesson: that is reflection, which is good. Looking back with a fear of being punished or being burdened with excessive guilt: that is rumination, which is unhelpful.

Rumination happens involuntarily, driven by the Nafs, meaning it happens without permission from your True Self (your Heart). It can get out of control and dominate you, which is when you ought to seek help because it can become illness like depression, anxiety or obsessive compulsive disorder. Reflection, by contrast, is an active process which you do quite deliberately, with a view to improving your awareness of yourself.

Okay, understood. But how about the future? Does the Muslim just let the future happen without caring for it?

Living for this moment, right, now, is all that we can actually control. If you are planning to live in a good way over the next few minutes, then you have described your future. As the future arrives, you act as well as you can, one second, one minute, one hour at a time.

You can and should, of course, plan things for tomorrow, because that helps you to get things done, and you can anticipate what risks and possibilities you face. Those who fail to plan, plan to fail! You live your life neither with careless disregard for the future, nor pointless fear of it. You live for now. You do what you have to do, adjusting your course accordingly with time.

The Muslim believes that everything is temporary, including life. But that does not mean he lives recklessly. The transient nature of life is a sign to the Muslim that he must tread gently and live as if a guest in his own body and on Earth, treating both with kindness.

The prophet is reported to have said "If anything befalls you, do not say, "If only I had done such-and-such, such a thing would have happened." Say instead, "It is the decree of Allah, and what He wills, He does," for saying "if only…" opens the way for Shaytan.'"

What about regret for sins of the past?

Ibn Masud reported that the Prophet PBUH said, "Regret is part of repentance."

Regret is different to being overwhelmed with guilt. Guilt feels dark and uncontrolled, while regret is a mindful, righteous experience. Regret can become guilt if one doesn't repent. As such, regret should be taken as part of remorse.

Guilt says, "My bad behaviour, proves I am a bad *person*". This is unhelpful. The idea of yourself as "bad" is central to guilt. Guilt is directed towards your identity, not your actions. It paralyses you from moving forward.

Remorse says, "My actions were not good, and I must double my efforts to not repeat them".
Remorse admits your actions were bad, but separates you the person from them. You did a bad thing, but that does not mean you are a bad person. This opens the door to moving forward.

Living more in the present moment

1. Endurance
If you are going for a run, or doing something that is getting you tired, let go of any worry about pain. At that moment, concentrate just on putting one leg in front of the other, literally one step at a time. You will find, almost always, that you are far less tired than your emotions are telling you. Do not over-exert yourself: if pain is sharp, deeply unpleasant, unusual or sudden, then stop.

2. Eating. Go and eat the smallest piece of fruit, the size of a raisin. Eat it very slowly, concentrating on every single little bit e and flavour. Make that experience large in your mind.

3. Breathing. If you are carried away at any moment, do the breathing cycle. Concentrate just on your breath, taking a breath in slowly, holding for ten seconds, then breathing out slowly, holding for ten more. Do a few cycles of this.

4. Find FLOW. Do something which makes you lose track of time. Be it reading a very pleasant du'aa, or drawing and craft, or cleaning. Just enjoy every part of that process, without concern about what time is passing.

5. Confronting. If something is looming in your mind, move towards it deliberately. Let it give you whatever feelings it does, and hear it out. Comfort yourself for the feelings: accept them, and offer solutions and wisdom for them as if you were helping a close friend out. Welcome difficulty.

Use this space for your own notes on the exercise opposite.

Instagram, March 2020

Forgetting the Positives

Thankfulness. An absolute cornerstone of the Muslim mind. The Prophet PBUH is reported to have said:

"Look at those who are less fortunate than yourselves, not at those who are better off than yourselves, so that you will not belittle the blessings that Allah has bestowed upon you" (Al-Mundhiri.)

How are Muslims thankful?

The Muslim has to pray five times daily. Each occasion has many parts where we acknowledge and thank God for giving us life and whatever blessings we have. More than that, even in day to day life, listen to Muslims' everyday words. Their conversations are overflowing with thankful notes and phrases. Some examples:

Mashallah means 'God has willed it' and is said as a mark of appreciation or praise when a Muslim sees something good.

Alhamdulillah means 'Praise be to God' and is said in a variety of situations, from when facing trials and difficulties right through to giving thanks for one's health or some other positive event.

Jazakallah means 'May God reward you with goodness' and is said when the Muslim is showing gratitude to someone else.

All roads and events lead the Muslim to a state of thankfulness of God.

Doesn't that lead them to feel indebted and helpless?

Indebtedness to Allah should be a good and positive feeling. The Muslim understands that God is much more merciful than he is punitive, and as such, that everything he has in life is a favour for him to use as well as he can. God encourages the Muslim to use everything he has in the path of something good. That would be a way of repaying the debt in a positive way, I suppose.

If a person feels over-burdened with a sense of being underserving, as if they don't deserve what they have and it feels like weighs heavily on their soul, then this is not indebtedness: this is needless guilt. This happens if the person fails to value himself as much as God does. It can also happen when the person is mentally unwell, in which case God has commanded him to seek remedy, and for those around him to help him.

Plenty of modern research shows that practising gratitude is helpful to relationships and wellbeing. In one study, a large group of people were trained to practice gratitude with prayer, a gratitude diary where they noted only the new things they were thankful for every day, and consciously going to thank others in their life. Compared to the people who didn't do this, the study group showed greater recollection of positive events, greater optimism for the future, and even had less physical problems, visiting their doctor less. Such is the power of thankfulness.

God is very fond of those recognise what he has given them. Not only does God give them more, but they also make use of what they have more creatively and constructively.

The original and best thankfulness habit is embedded in our prayers daily: our salah, our remembrance of Allah, reading Quran, and in our du'aa. Take a time to make a special mention of the things that you want to thank Allah for when you pray next. Be very specific in what you thank him for. It doesn't matter how insignificant the thing is: if it is in your life, you must find a reason to see why it is good for you, and thank God for putting it there.

Some people find it useful to start a thankfulness diary. That sounds a bit more than what it really is. It can just be a few words, every morning, that you type into your phone or onto am piece of paper, where you note down three new things every day that you are thankful for. Try it for a month.

You would think that you might run out of things to be thankful for. But if you do this right, it actually works the other way round. The more you thank God for, the more you realise you have to be thankful for. It is an immensely uplifting and self-acknowledging experience, which is proven to improve happiness within as little as two weeks.

Mind Training Box: Thankfulness

Your happiness will increase dramatically and rapidly if you do any one the following easy things.

1. **Alhamdulillah.** Practice praising Allah in your mind every few seconds, and then *justify* it. You stood up- alhamdulillah for your legs. You saw a tree- alhamdulillah for nature. You remembered a friend- alhamdulillah for your having a friend, and for your memory. Make it a game with children, like the I-spy game: *"**Alhamdulillah, so thankful we are, for something beginning with... "***

2. **The Shoebox.** Get a shoebox and every day, write a tiny note of something you are thankful for, and put it in there. Open it after a month.

3. **The Sticky-note Wall.** Choose a wall or a fridge door, and get a pad of small post-its. Everyone in the family must write one thing every day to put on the wall, until it is full.
That day, everyone sits round and reads the notes together.

4. **The Letter of thanks**
Write a detailed hand-written letter to a person you are grateful to have in your life. Be detailed. Express all the wonderful qualities about this person, and how they personally have affected your life for the better. Deliver it by hand if you can.

5. **The Whatsapp thank you bomb**
Go through all your Whatsapp contacts. For each one, remember something you can thank them for. Tell them in a few words that *'I was just reminiscing, and I remembered how you .... I am still thankful for that! That's all. Keep well, Wassalaam:)'*

Use this space for your own notes on the exercise opposite.

Practice Being Thankful.
This is the face of a man who got cleared, after spending 17 years in jail for a murder he didn't commit.

From ' Ways to Make Peace with Yourself'
Page 91-106, Instant Insights

drtkharris.wordpress.com

Teaching Children Thankfulness

<u>Muslim version of I-Spy!</u>
Like this:
"Alhamdulillah,
How thankful we are,
For something beginning
with …(whatever letter the
item begins with)."

Asking for clues:
You have to ask *why you are*
thankful for that thing.

120

Being afraid of fear itself

Life is full of anxiety: it is part of the normal psychological experience. It might be unpleasant, but the Muslim accepts its unpleasantness as he accepts any other thing.

Why does the Muslim believe anxiety and fear exist? Why would God give people such things?

It is not for the Muslim to find a firm answer as to why God does anything at all. God's actions and intentions for our lives are not available to us to interpret with certainty. Sure, we know some of what he likes and doesn't, and we obey his rules, but we avoid getting bogged down in the idea of *why* to the point of obsession, because we are told that this is not for us to truly know.

However, we are still encouraged to understand the world in a physical sense. God has told the Muslim, for example, that there is a *duality* to everything. There is benefit in some bad things just as much as there is danger in some good things.

We believe that emotions serve many functions, mostly connected to helping us to navigate the world in a safe or secure way. Sure, they can get out of hand. However, they do have their use, in moderation. We interpret some things as unpleasant but that does not mean they are automatically bad.

Anxiety, pain, fear- how could they ever be good?

When it is in normal amounts, any emotion can focus or deter the mind in a helpful way. Think of something like pain. Pain is unpleasant, but it has a good function. If you burn your fingers on a stove, the pain makes you withdraw your hand from the heat. Without that pain, you would have done yourself more damage.

With too much pain, though, particularly long term pain like back pain, it serves little apparent function to a scientific mind, but to a Muslim, that back pain, as useless as it might seem, is there serving some kind of purpose which is unseen and unknowable. If he didn't have the pain, for example, then maybe he would have gone outside and got very badly hurt. We cannot know. We must do whatever we can to reduce it, but beyond that, we bear even chronic pain with grace. There is much blessing in tolerating that which we cannot change.

Then why would the Muslim ever make effort to get rid of difficulty?

There used to be the type of thinking that we must endure difficulties or situations without making effort to avoid them, and even inflict pain upon ourselves in order to earn God's favour, but that was really when some people lost their way. The Muslim of today has rediscovered the Hadith that order him to seek relief from things which burden him, because the Prophet and God himself have told us that we ought to seek relief and comfort from difficulty, and take an easier path if we can find it: the path of *Ih'san*.

The problem will last exactly as long as God has ordained it to last. The Muslim just has to find a way to manage it whilst it is there.

With anxiety, we find that it waxes and wanes just like the waves in the sea. As a temporary emotion, it is not to be feared or dismissed. Rather, we ought to let it come in to the mind, listen to what it has to say, and let it go of its own accord. It will do so if we are kind to ourselves in this way.

The point of this chapter is to help you understand that there is a value to every experience and phenomenon, good, bad or otherwise. Contentment lies in revising your expectations to accept these things as part of the furniture of life. Sometimes, you find a way round them, other times, you have to put up with them because your efforts to defeat them have not worked out. Most of them will just dissolve away.

Life is a mix of successes and failures. We are better off *turning up to life* because at least then we are actually living it. You might experience more unpleasantness than the next person, but that does not mean you have more *opportunities for misery*. It's *how* you accept events, good or bad, that determines your level of contentment.

Mind Training Session for this chapter: See the Sessions in RIADH, self acceptance, and Islamic meditation.

Instagram, March 2020

Not keeping our cool when provoked

So, given that we acknowledge that even unpleasant experiences have a purpose, the Muslim is told that she ought to accept it and deal with it in a way that sees her suffer to a minimum.

With this in mind, we can use whatever techniques seem to work within the limits of what we can do. The first one is a very useful technique, called the RIADH. The word 'RIADH' means 'Garden of Peace' in Arabic. It forms a useful acronym for the steps in this technique.

A Riadh in Turkey

Imagine emotions to be a storm cloud. The cloud is approaching your garden at great speed. How do you prepare for such an amount of rain all at once? If you are feeling unpleasant emotions and would like to reduce their hold on you, the more you practice this technique the better it works. Following the R-I-A-D-H steps:

a) Recognise

Name it, and say it to yourself. 'This is anger', 'This is guilt' and so on. Recognise that you are being visited by emotion. Whatever the emotion, if it is strong then you need to give it a name and recognition. That immediately helps calm it.

b) Inhale

In the second garden, you inhale, slowly and deeply. Use all your chest and belly. This sends soothing signals to your emotional centres in the base of the brain. It is astonishing how much slow breathing can actually calm the mind. Just concentrate on the breathing, for a couple of minutes. Your mind and body are your duty and priority.

c) Accept

The third garden is the garden of acceptance. Even unpleasant emotions must be accepted. You don't need to know why the emotion is there. Make peace with what is within you. It is in your garden, and it is part of you. You shouldn't fight a cloud, it is simply bringing rain. Accept the rain, both gentle and stormy. This way, it doesn't have a hold of you. You don't need to act on emotions them. Just hold fast and mots of them will just pass by.

d) Du'aa- Say Alhamdulillah!

Thank Allah for your emotions, use them if they are useful, but just let them pass if they are not. Storm-clouds can have good or bad effects, just like your emotions. Welcoming them is a way of dealing with them calmly. Be thankful that you are designed in a way that is perfect in the way Allah intended.

e) Happiness

The happiness pool is at at the centre of the garden. This is where the rain can fall and drain away. Emotions drain away; the wave has passed. You can now move on; the waters are calm. Get on with what you were doing before the emotion came to disturb you.

If you have practised the method enough, you will probably be feeling a lot more settled by now. If not, then it doesn't matter. Emotions are only emotions. Take it easy on yourself. No need to be hard on yourself for not getting it perfect or suddenly becoming ecstatically happy. These things take time. The brain is a very *plastic* entity, meaning it changes slowly, over weeks and months, when you practice something, becoming steadily better the more you do it. Be patient; many of the best things in life come after we make the effort, and take things day by day without expecting miracles.

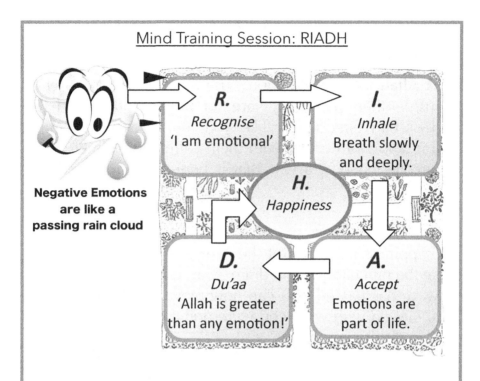

Practise the steps again and again, every time you are about to react emotionally to something. RIADH is a special place that interrupts and settles your mind's natural emotional dramas.

If you can't recognise when you have been emotional, think about a time when you felt compelled to say something to someone because you had to win an argument, or tell them off. Or when you got told off and felt awful. That's an example right there. Re-imagine that moment, and take the steps again.

Recognise – Inhale – Accept – Du'aa – Happiness

Use this space for your own notes on the exercise opposite.

Both laziness and overwork
Are mistakes which cause us pain.

Lazy people and workaholics: same problem

Some people neglect hard work, while others overdo it. Either way is unwise. The Muslim is instructed to work, and to have a balanced work ethic. Here's an example:

Then Prophet PBUH said
"—if someone goes out to seek nourishment for his small children, he is in the way of Allah. And if he works for his old father and mother he is in the way of Allah. And if he works for himself for modesty, it is in the way of Allah, but if he works for the purpose of pride and boasting, he is in the way of Satan". [Tabarani]

Clearly, people need to earn a living. A person is obliged to participate in permissible things like business and employment.

Does a Muslim hold work above all else?

The Muslim is not convinced that work is a salvation in itself. He must seek work, and try his hand at business he wishes, but the success of his efforts is up to Allah.

Most importantly, what the chapter really means is that the Muslim does not put employed work or business as the prime source of worth. Other roles in life- as a father, mother, sister, or brother, supporting loved ones with kind words, consideration, giving them due time and attention and helping them to thrive- this is also our work, and if we neglect it, the consequences are worse than skipping employed work.

Too many people, men especially, believe that their work is the beginning and the end of their contribution to their family, expecting that the wife and children will be fine just with monetary income. They don't take time to show love and interest in their children's learning, or resolving issues that come up in the family. This leaves many families, wealthy and poor, to be emotionally and morally starved.

How many times do we see rich fathers whose sons show no respect for their wealth? How many times do we see children grow up with all the comforts of life but without guidance on what makes a good character? You cannot expect to throw money at a problem that requires your presence and nurturance. It just means you will have bigger problems, and wealth becomes a useless or even dangerous thing in the hands of people who lack insight.

So what exactly is the value of work for the Muslim?

Islam places a good value on work. The Quran says

"That man can have nothing but what he strives for; That (the fruit of) his striving will soon come in sight: Then will he be rewarded with a reward complete." (53:39-41)

In Islam, work is given special importance to the extent that it is even considered as an act of worship. But one must be careful to balance one's obligations. Work is certainly not equal to the value of caring for family.

How about those who spend their time in worship?

If they worship at the expense of work that must be done, they are misguided. The prophet Isa (Jesus) once saw a man who was completely devoted to worship. When he asked the man how he got his bread, he said that he relied on his brother, who worked, to provide it for him. Isa replied "then your brother is more religious than you are".

We know that the Prophet PBUH disliked those who hoarded wealth, earning without giving. His life was always spent in a mix of things, from business to prayer, meditation and leisure, but above work, he loved the company of his family and friends, and was a source of emotional nourishment for them. He paid close attention to his various roles, never letting work or business overtake. This is the way.

The hazards of blind obsession with work and career are also described well in modern scientific enquiry. For mental wellbeing, people who invest too highly in their career are vulnerable to nervous breakdowns, depression and addiction.

This is thought to happen because of the fallout from getting too much of your self worth from things outside your control, and from the mistake of comparing one's successes with others.

The idea of security in work is also a myth. It has become clear over the years that a person's career can disappear for reasons that are not his fault at all. From a downturn in the market to the actions of a jealous coworker, many hazards await the blindly earnest worker. Achievement is empty if one does not also earn security or steadiness of character from their achievement.

In summary, we have duties to work on many things. Being obsessed with work for the sake of income is a danger to be avoided because we risk overvaluing it at the expense of our other very real duties in life. You can neglect your work and the most that might happen is you lose your job. Neglect your family and Deen, however, and your character, relationships and future will suffer.

Work is essential towards a sound purpose,
such as feeding one's family, and for the sake of Allah.

Putting Work in its place

This session is a 'thought experiment' for the reader who is very involved in his or her work/career. Supposing you became disabled and were unable to work. You have children to feed and look after too.

Keep asking: 'what's the worst that could happen?'

(WTWTCH?)	*We would have to live off savings*
WTWTCH?	*We would run out of savings*
WTWTCH?	*We would risk becoming homeless*
WTWTCH?	*My parents would accommodate us*
WTWTCH?	*They would get old and pass away*
WTWTCH?	*We would starve. Nobody would help*
WTWTCH?	*I would pass away*
WTWTCH?	*That's it I guess. Allah would make me shaheed for starving.*
WTWTCH?	*My children would suffer and die*
WTWTCH?	*They would become shaheed too.*
WTWTCH?	*All very unpleasant, but with a righteous end. Allah sees all. Trust Him!*

This works for any issue that has a tight hold over you.
You would rather be on your deathbed having given an excess of love and attention to your loved ones, than to have worked too much at your business or job. Work is a source of sustenance, and adds some meaning to life. Not more than that. Do your best, but not to the expense of your finest efforts, which should be for people who matter, and for Allah.

136

Use this space for your own notes on the exercise opposite.

The wise Muslim knows this:
Discussions are an exchange of wisdom,
and arguments are an exchange of ignorance.

Communication Skills Get Rusty

If one understands the Muslim mind, one can become surprisingly adept at communicating with others. Let me demonstrate. The Muslim mind is in three parts, right?

Nafs (Ego), **Intellect**, and **Heart** (True Self).

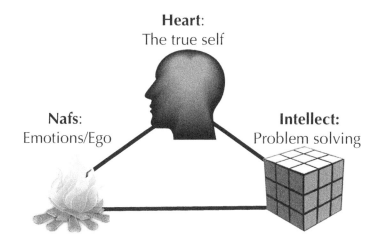

Heart:
The true self

Nafs:
Emotions/Ego

Intellect:
Problem solving

Well, we can use this model when we consider how to communicate with someone. When anyone expresses themselves, they are expressing one or more of these parts. Listening and watching for which one, allows us to understand them better.

If they are emotional, or talking about such things pride, ego, loyalty, shame and so on, the Nafs is active, so they are speaking from there. If they are trying to be logical or cooperative with a group, or solve problems with facts and planning, then the Intellect is active. If they are trying to show higher judgment, restraint of emotion, or generally being dignified, compassionate and wise, namely their best self, then it is the Heart at play. When we work out which part they are speaking from, we can react in a way that is appropriate.

A person speaking from their Nafs does not respond easily to cold logic. They respond to *non verbal* things such as eye contact, facial expression, close attention, smiling, and empathy.

A person being very logical and detached would respond better to you if you are similarly focussed on evidence, facts, plans, and cooperation.

Finally, a person who is being their highest self, in tune with their Heart, is clearly someone who is quite pleasant to be around, because they are speaking in the wisest way, listening to their own Intellect and Ego, and judging how to pose their conversation to us in the best way.

In composing a message to someone, they hear us along those same three channels as well. Their Nafs will be listening to the emotional appeal of our message, our body language and so on. Their Intellect will be looking at the facts and truths in it, and the Heart will be trying to forge a wiser path than either, adding in experience and judgment.

Never argue with a fool.
He thinks he is doing the same thing.

Do when calm what you said you would do when angry;
you will quickly learn the value of keeping quiet.

The good Muslim shines in a way that
lets others see themselves in a good light.

Allah has given us two ears and one mouth
so we can listen twice as much as we speak.

Reflect on the way people communicate

People are more often drawn to emotions and instincts than to facts. The Nafs (Ego) that dominates communications in the world around us. It is the most rapid, and unfortunately often the strongest part of people's decision process. Look at these traits of the Nafs or Ego:

Danger sensitivity. Irrationally attentive to bad news.
Possessions. Needing to have nice things.
Sex appeal. To prefer messages promising seduction.
Conformity. The wish to be like others.
Similarity. Being suspicious of those who are different.
Security. To live protected from unknown dangers.
Cleverness. Portray oneself as intelligent or sophisticated.
Impulsivity. To act on emotional appeal, without thought.
Perfectionism. Aspire to be, and like things, that are perfect
Nurturance. To show love for those who are helpless/ weak
Recognition. To be prized or noticed positively by others.
Superiority. To be better than others in some way
Victory. To resolve issues by competition and conflict
Certainty. To prefer that which is known and safe.
Novelty. To be curious about the weird and unusual.
Loyalty. To demand allegiance in exchange for protection
Face. To be sensitive to when one might appear humiliated

Look at the news, politics, social media, or advertising to see how they rely on the Nafs. Also look at the people you deal with- how much are they reliant on their Nafs? Few people have the presence of mind to speak with their Heart or even their Intellect most of the time. Aspire to be more like this.

142

Use this space for your own notes on the exercise opposite.

Communication is something most people learn naturally.
Some of us really struggle with it. We all can learn to improve.

Persuading and Influencing

This chapter is itself a mind training session.
Everyone wants to be more persuasive. Unfortunately, the ones who do it best are those who use it to trick or deceive. This chapter is here as an effort to reclaim that. It is true that 'nice' people tend not to ask for what they want as much as they should, hence you should read on. Learn how to persuade.

The basic secret for persuasion is two fold:
a) You are not convincing one person. You are convincing their three different minds. Each part of the mind demands a slightly different strategy if it is to be persuaded.
b) Make the change seem like their idea: the more they talk about change, the more they are persuaded.

Persuading the Nafs or Ego.

If in doubt, the Nafs is the most direct target of any persuasion effort. This is because the Nafs is normally the most rapid and often the strongest force in someone: people react emotionally before they do intellectually.

These are the main factors that work with the Nafs:

1. **Visual, auditory, sensory.** The Nafs is persuaded by the senses. Appeal to their bias towards appearances and other sensory inputs (smell, touch etc) by taking care in your appearance, and using smell and touch in a way that fits the person, the culture and the occasion. Getting this right often wins a person over right from the beginning.

2. **Conforming.** Describe how many other people have taken up your offer and fund it successful. Use knowledge of people familiar or similar to them if you can.

3. **Urgency.** Create a sense of time running out. Scarcity of opportunity makes people act more decisively to seize something that may otherwise disappear.

4. **Similarity.** Understand and emphasise in what ways you and they are similar, sharing outlooks on the world. Similarity breeds comfort and agreement.

5. **Familiarity.** Personalise the encounter. Reveal something warm and personal about yourself, creating a conversation that is mutually disclosing. It's harder for someone to say no to you if they feel they know you more than a stranger.

6. **Fear of not changing.** Get them to describe what they are unhappy about with the current state of affairs, then to try to get them to go on to describe how your offer might be of use in reducing that unhappiness. This creates a sense of discomfort (cognitive dissonance) that makes them want to fix the issue.

7. **Reciprocation.** Ask them to do you a small favour that they would find easy to accomplish. Thank them immensely when they do so. This creates a mindset where they feel valued, and they become more inclined to agree with other things you suggest.

It is often said that to know what a person wants you should look to see what choices they have already made, and go along with those choices. If a chap comes in to a clothes store, the canny salesman will to direct him towards the type of clothing that he is already wearing. Again, whatever you do, your intentions must be honest and good.

<u>Persuading the Intellect</u>

Here's how to engage another's intellect:

1. **Credibility.** Have credibility and authority on whatever it is you are trying to convince someone about. Demonstrate your knowledge or qualification in a straightforward way. They are more likely to take your message on if they think you have understood the matter deeply.

2. **Logic.** Create a logical reason as to why they would be better off with what you have to offer. Logic and reason are always better in convincing people, but we overestimate their utility generally. The Nafs dominates as a default.

3. **Dispassionate detachment.** Create the impression that you are indifferent to what choice they make. This gives them a sense that what you have really is valuable, and that they need to decide themselves. This gives them logical authority and ownership of the decision, which is a fair and powerful thing.

Persuading other peoples' Heart / True Self

If a person appears wise, restrained and discerning, their Heart is strong. This is the hardest to fool, so don't bother if you don't really believe in yourself. You will fail. This is where being genuine is the only way.

1. **Be yourself.**　show little interest in persuading them; rather, just get to know them a bit more.

2. **Their needs.** Ask them to describe what benefits they would gain from taking your offer up. This gives them the chance to sell it to themselves.

3. **Stories and truths.** Tell them a genuine story about someone who took the offer and gained their success, or avoided disaster, because of their wise choice. The story must be real, and relatable. success, or avoidance of disaster, that is relatable and describes why the offer is such a good idea.

4. **Let the matter rest.** A good True Self tends to think something over and reflect on the quality of their decisions. You have only to let them know you are interested in helping them and that you are someone worth listening to. If they believe you, you will have no problem winning their favour but it only comes from repeatedly showing yourself to be of service and assistance.

If you don't know which part of the person is listening, it can feel like you're talking a different language.

**Striving for excellence will do you good.
Striving for perfection will make you ill.**

Confusing Excellence with Perfectionism

Excellence is doing your best. Perfectionism is silly. The Muslim is immune to the delusion that people must strive endlessly and ruthlessly towards some kind of perfect peak of anything, be it religion, skill, or habit. In fact, he is actively discouraged from it. Only Allah can be perfect, so the Muslim is warned against trying to do anything to those extreme standards. Why attempt to compete with God?

A Muslim strives towards improvement with the principle of *Ih'san,* a word meaning a combination of ease and goodness. The Muslim understands *Ih'san* to be a way where he tries to be good across the board, without exhausting his efforts in any one area.

Psychologically this makes great sense. For wellbeing, we are encouraged to have a rich and diverse life where we don't obtain our pleasures or self-esteem excessively from any one particular area. It's about balance.

Psychologists tell us that perfectionism is a damaging trait to live by, because it is never achievable, and if we pursued it, we would just become fixated, failed, and exhausted. We end up viewing the world in intolerant terms, either perfect or not, either good or bad. This leaves us prone to a host of problems such as conflict with others, isolation, and anxiety and depression.

For training, see Challenging Negativity.

**Whether they deserve forgiveness or not,
Forgive them because you deserve peace.**

Forgiveness and Grudges

After every single prayer, the Muslim is told to forgive anyone of their transgressions against him, and to seek forgiveness from those whom he may have let down.

Islam places great importance on keeping a peaceful community, so much so that if two people are arguing in the mosque, a Muslim is even, remarkably, permitted to lie, if the lie diffuses the situation. For a religion that has got such a false hard-line reputation in media circles, this might surprise many people.

People who bear grudges form beliefs about the world which centre around having been forsaken in some way. This is both damaging to both mental and physical health.

Research tells us that people who hold on to negative emotions, and who don't express positive ones, are more likely to have a poor immune response. This happens through a chain of hormonal and chemical pathways, leading the person's body unable to identify cancer cells when they form. They face, literally, a greater cancer risk.

Furthermore, it is exhausting to bear grudges. The constant stressed state of a grudge-bearer causes impaired glucose functioning, leading to weight problems or diabetes, and also to poor handling of fats, leading to fatty deposits in arteries- coronary artery and other vascular disorders.

The grudge-bearer is already preoccupied with his anger or resentment, and is also more prone to breakdown when other life events happen.

Islam is quite firm on this issue: the Muslim is not just encouraged to dismiss a grudge, but he is required to do so. God tells the Muslim directly that God is merciful to the person who is merciful, and God is forgiving to those who are forgiving. God refrains from showing mercy to those who bear grudges and don't let go. The Muslim is told to ask for forgiveness even if he doesn't expect that his forgiveness will be granted from the other.

Doesn't all this forgiving make Muslims more prone to being taken advantage of again?

Not if you keep in mind that the Muslim has to be alert to the nature of man. Man is prone to deception, errors, and conflict, and man is likely to repeat the same errors. Being of a forgiving nature does not give the Muslim permission to put himself in the same position again. God makes it clear that he is to learn from his experiences. If the dog bit you once, you must expect it will do so again, and it's on you of you think it won't.

Ask Allah's help in helping you to let go of a grudge, or before you seek forgiveness from a person you have let down.

Let it go. Forgive, forget, and accept

The thing that's bothering you. Will it be of importance in 5 years? If not, then let it go. If yes, then can you do anything about it today? Then do it. If you can't, let it go. Let it go!

If you have upset someone, you are going to ask them for forgiveness. Don't panic. Start of by writing down a short note to them. It will help if you give it to them, but *you don't to*. Writing it itself will help you to feel more at peace.

Dear ……
I am sorry that I upset you when ……

Please forgive me for this. I really hope you can. I regret what happened, and I acknowledge my part in it.

I am also willing to put things right, by ………………

If there is anything you would like me to do to put things right, let me know.

Make peace with yourself: acknowledge if the anger or upset is still there, because you are human. Just try to be gentle with yourself, allowing the feeling to drip away over time as it definitely will, inshallah.
If you are upset because someone let you down, think deeply about how this grudge will hurt you more than it does them.

Use this space for your own notes on the exercise opposite.

Instagram, March 2020

158

Depriving the Mind of its Sunlight: *Learning*

God tells the Muslim to keep learning. A great importance is placed on it:

"Say: My Lord, increase me in knowledge."
Quran 20:114

Seeking facts and truths is part of the Intellect's job.

For those who keep their intellect focussed on learning something, we notice a measured effect on their wellbeing. The effect is not related to what is being learned, as long as the person is interested in it, and it is worthwhile material. The effect is in fact related to the *process of learning itself*.

In the brain, the best learning happens *associatively*. That means that the mind takes a subject or a fact, and goes on a walk round what it already knows: the memory, a person's experience, an emotional response, a sense of humour, where you were when you learned it, what mood you were in, and so on.

Memory is not like a list, but more like a spiderweb of connections. The finer and stronger the web is woven, the more expert the person becomes, and within this we see a curious increase in positive neurotransmitters. This is called *zeal*: a state of intense well-being when someone is involved in the learning to a deep degree.

Besides this, learning does help a person to gain one important box in the wellbeing table: Mastery.

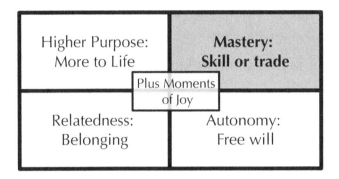

Mastery is when a person is in command of something that is their particular skill, their thing. It could be cooking, cleaning, painting, science, finance, anything which gives the person a sense of value with respect to their community.

Show me a demonstration of exceptional learning power.

A person was once bed bound and mute, unable to feed himself, communicating only in screams and noises, unable to even get out of bed. Slowly, he taught himself to walk. Within time, he also taught himself to speak, from scratch. All of this, with no specific teaching, no books, no teachers.

This is the story of almost every human being on earth. It's story of the baby! If you learned as a baby, you can certainly do it as an adult. God has told you to seek knowledge, so it follows that he has given you the ability to learn.

160

Remember this. Your aim is to try to have fun while learning. Happiness and contentment are better found in *the act*, not the *outcome*. It does not matter whether you actually are successful in learning the skill or subject. It matters that you just embark on it.

Here's a simple task. The Japanese word for thank you is 'Arigato'. Say it out loud. A-ri-ga-to. Now imagine there is a Japanese person in front of you, who has given you some nice food. Thank them. Arigato. You have started learning another language. Babies learn language by listening, imitating, one word at a time. They forget, mumble, get frustrated, laugh, and mess around with pronunciation. Take your cue from them.

It is a myth to say that adults are not capable of learning like they once were when children. It's just that we don't take it for how it should be. We take learning to be dry, rote-fashion, focussing on what we got wrong more than what we got right. No wonder people shy away from it. Learning can be difficult and challenging but it is best if it is a relaxed and positive process. Learn anything with experiment, imagination, and concentrate on the moments of happiness at the smallest achievement.

Learn, or relearn, something

You can learn anything you like, from gardening to driving to astronomy. If you are restricted to the home or for money, learning a new language is an especially good, because it is easily available, and it helps train thought processing. There are so many free sites online (e.g. Duolingo), and so many videos where you can see people talking any language you can name. In the end it doesn't matter what you learn. The benefit to your wellbeing comes from the *effort*.

What are you going to learn? Pick something instinctive and fun, which piques your interest. Try, and then drop it if you lose interest. Be unafraid to try something else.

When can you learn? Add 'Learning' as part to your daily planner for an hour or two. Maybe 5 hours a week.

Set an aim, every day or every session, for what you want to know by the end of that session.
What is your aim today?
Did you celebrate your achievement today? You must.
Could you find someone to learn with you? It helps.
Can you connect to a community of similar folk? Do so.
Did you thank God for your chance to fulfil his command by learning something? Do it. Tell him you are grateful.

Finally, and very importantly, this:
Did you forget part or all of what you learned? I hope so. It's a sign of being normal. It doesn't matter if you succeed or fail. The benefit comes from the *effort* of learning.

Use this space for your own notes on the exercise opposite.

It's foolish to keep questioning everything.
Accept that you will never have all the answers.
Even the camera can never be sure of what it sees.

The Madness of WHY WHY WHY

If you are in some emotional fix, you might reasonably be hunting down the reasons for why you're in that state. If something bad happened to you, you might be wondering how it happened, why it did, and what could have prevented it.

If you are troubled by these things and getting nowhere, you are in the grip of a useless pattern of thought. Originally, it was reasonable to reflect, because you could find out causes and prevent future mistakes. But now, it's all just going round and round.

Emotions are often just plain irrational. There is often no real reason why they hang around, or even come up, sometimes. This is the nature of the Nafs. Accept that you won't find an answer, and make peace with the emotion without questioning it. Just let it be.

You don't need answers if you decide to just be OK with your emotions being as crazy as they are. Why fight a very strong natural force? You don't have to react to it. Just let it be. If you are really in an emotional fix, try the Garden of Peace methods from earlier in the book. If you are trying to come to terms with something rude or incomprehensible that others have done to upset you, look at the next Action Page.

Obsessional thoughts- called *wasawis* in Arabic- are part of normal psychological life. How often can one be sat at a table and experience a sudden idea, a fancy, to spill all the food everywhere, or to get up and shout an obscenity. Believe it or not, this is normal thought!

Most people can dismiss these things as part of the trifles of a healthy mind churning away as it does, but for those who don't, it is often reassuring and calming enough to know that these unwanted thoughts are just thoughts which they do not need to act out, and which they won't act out especially if they find them very distasteful or bizarre. People can be reminded of the fact that they retain their free will to control their actions, even if their thoughts are unwelcome.

The nature, content, severity, and influence of wasawis vary from one person to the other. For some, they only cause mild anxiety and worry, while for others may be more severely affected to the point of becoming spiritually, mentally, emotionally, psychologically, and socially incapacitated.

In addition to the next action page, remember one special thing: read Quran. It is often a very powerful, sensible and psychologically effective solution for times when people feel blighted by unwelcome thoughts. Besides being very pleasing to Allah, reading Quran provides both *activity* and *consolation*.

166

Many people find reading Quran to be a
deeply peaceful and calming activity. Alhamdulillah.

Dismiss hurtful and unwanted thoughts

a) Realise that other peoples' rudeness is not about you. Their behaviour is more a reflection of their own issues and preoccupations.

b) Consider less personal explanations. If someone doesn't greet you, maybe they're just shy or preoccupied.

c) Welcome criticism; thank the criticizer. If it was meant well, you come across as someone who is open and reflective. If not, then that's their problem. Win win.

d) Imagine if another person was in the same situation. How would you calm them and advise them to conduct themselves? Give yourself the same advice.

e) Accept this Truth: that you can't please everyone.

f) Accept that criticisms and failures are just passing events.

To stop thoughts from circulating, try these steps:

 Notice the thought. Acknowledge it's there.

 Say STOP. Raise your hand/imagine a stop sign.

 Tackle the thought. See 'Challenge Negativity'.

 Breathe slowly. Distract yourself. Move on.

Use this space for your own notes on the exercise opposite.

Confidence is from humble preparation and effort, and knowing that all else is in the hands of Allah.

Lacking Confidence Before a Big Event

Confidence is about trying your best on any given day.
It is **not** about being good at something. You put in the effort, but God creates the result. If you turn out to be good, that's fine. If not, that's fine too. It was always thus, and always will be.

Many of the greatest over-achievers are actually not confident at all: in fact, they seem to work harder precisely because they don't believe they are good enough. They muddle through their insecurity by over-compensating, trying hard without a sense of knowing they are OK. This isn't great for their sense of well-being. Their achievements come at a great cost to other things in their life, like relationships, Deen and so on.

Confidence is how good you feel you might be at something. *Competence* is how good you actually might be. The two things are independent of one another. Someone can have neither, either, or both. It is true to say, though, that people who are generally more confident about things are happier in life, and achieve better as a whole.

Confidence is troublesome when people worry about being good at something. This causes a lot of anxiety. Confidence comes from doing your reasonable best without going crazy about it. It is not about being good as such. Forget about the result. Just try to get each little step right, and if you fail, that's fine. Failure is an event, not a person.

<u>Gain confidence before a task</u>

1. Calm your nerves. Try this breathing exercise.

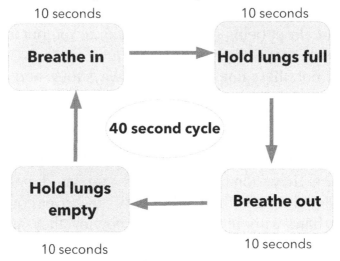

2. Excite and inspire yourself.

Positive affirmations are things you tell yourself to feel good. You are strong! Allah is on your side. Success is assured. Remember, state, and assert your strengths.

Seek inspiration from a favourite speaker, or from a mentor or person of respect. There are plenty of very positive and encouraging speakers online; our own Mufti Menk is a great example. Find an encouraging speech. Learn it. Repeat it.

Use this space for your own notes on the exercise opposite.

**Choose between two pains:
The pain of self-restraint,
or the pain of regret.**

Behaving or Talking without Restraint

The Muslim prefers to not say something at all, rather than blurt something out. The Muslim prefers to not show any emotion at all if there is a risk that his emotion will be misinterpreted. This is not denial of emotion, so much as cautious, benevolent restraint.

Broadly speaking, we over-react to everything, all the time. This is the nature of our Nafs- our ego and emotions are so.

If you find yourself indulging in anything too much, Ramadan is the one time when you have to practice restraint. It is instrumental in uniting all Muslims with the value of self restraint. However, to benefit from it completely you must learn that it is not just about avoiding food and drink. It is about delaying self gratification in all physical needs.

Our better qualities are sometimes shy, hiding from our daily selves. There is a great amount of our character and strength that hides in the recesses, waiting for us to be quieter, emerging when we show humble self restraint. If we adopt it for long enough, those good qualities start to show themselves. We learn more about ourselves, and feel blessed.

What about injustice in front of our eyes? Wouldn't the Muslim believe in trying to resolve it?

There is a difference between *reactionism* and *activism*. Activism is permissible when Muslim believes that something must be done to change the way something is happening in her society. She relies on his Heart (her wisdom and beliefs), and her Intellect. The two things together enable the Muslim to speak up for her values, and do what she needs to do to be influential enough to make the change.

But peoples' feelings don't respond to logic. How could a Muslim convince people to change if she doesn't acknowledge their feelings?

You are right. People do behave in a rather primitive or emotional manner when they are in large crowds or factions. The Muslim is aware that people behave more from their Nafs, but to react with his own Nafs would worsen the issue. One Nafs against another is likely to lead to a battle for superiority through strength: a conflict of violent words or actions, which is always a very last resort.

But we digress. We're talking about restraint. We're talking about de-involving yourself from things that you believe you need, but you tend to over-use. Remember also that the Muslim must be restrained in his everyday actions, not just Ramadan or on the Mondays and Thursdays that the Prophet PBUH fasted on. Fasting days are times when we focus on restraint, in the hope that it rubs off on the rest of our time. It requires refreshing frequently, this is among the great benefits of why we do it at least one month a year.

Instagram, March 2020

177

Practise self-restraint

Every year Muslims have the glorious gift of a bootcamp of combat training. The opponent: temptation and lack of inhibition. A tricky thing to deal with, but the gift of fasting liberates strengths from us which otherwise hide in the shadows or our louder indulgence. See it as much more than just missing the food out. Additionally, it is a Sunnah to fast on Mondays and Thursdays.

Looking into the fast more deeply, we find that it is not just about avoiding food. It is also about restraint of all the other needs.

The tongue: Speak less, or not at all. Let people know you are trying to observe the fast with minimal talking.
The eyes: Avoid looking at indulgences such as social media or entertainment.
The ears: Prefer silence, solitude, and humility.
The body: Restrict your movements to a quiet, more secluded space if you can. Be gentler and less vigorous, exerting finer control.

If you have trouble speaking out too much, or always acting out of turn, there is great insight to be gained by deliberately withdrawing for a short period. Consider working with a shaykh if your Madhab is fine with this, or if not, try it on your own.

Practice Muraqabah (Islamic mindfulness)- periods when you are silent and just listen to your own self.

Practice I'tikaaf- the self-restriction of the last ten days of Ramadan. Reward yourself after each fast with a small treat, and thank Allah for the presence of mind that you will inevitably gain.

Use this space for your own notes on the exercise opposite.

**We barely control our own behaviour;
why should we expect others to control theirs better?**

Disappointed Expectations, Blurred Boundaries.

The very word Muslim, besides meaning a follower of Islam, means literally 'one who has submitted and is at peace'.

It is a commonly known even outside the Muslim world, that the Muslims say,"Whatever happens, it is the will of Allah." This is quite apt, and it has a sound basis.

Letting go of things one cannot control is a cornerstone of inner peace. Muslims are aware of how little control human beings really over life at all. A Muslim controls what he is entitled to and what is appropriate to control. The rest is to be left to Allah.

The happy and content Muslim takes into account the reality: the weather, prevailing mood, or likeliness of change, in the things around her that she cannot change. Then she forms a plan of action that works with this reality. Not being able to control things does not mean that you should forget about them.

The Muslim knows that you adjust to what happens in life, or else you will find yourself angry and confused as to why things don't happen the way you want.

If you find that something keeps going round and round in your mind and you can't let go of it no matter how you try, then ask yourself if it is actually helpful, or if it is getting in the way of your day and harming you. If that, then seek help! Happiness is based on making peace with your reality, not on your expectations. Pick on a problem that you have, and accept its reality rather than your expectations of it.

Supposing you have a very difficult neighbour. You are in a feud over something, and no matter how you have tried, you can't resolve it. It's causing you a lot of misery. Look at your expectations.

They include things like
'I should get on with my neighbours'
'I should be able to resolve an argument'
'My neighbour is so unreasonable. I wish he would just go away.'
'I get on with everyone else. It's him who's at fault'.
'I'm on the right side of the law/ common sense/ morality'.

Knowing this, you see where the problem lies. Lots of expectations. We are much better off not expecting the world to behave according to our ideals. We take people as we find them; we are friendly and courteous and principled, inviting the same but not *expecting* it.

Boundaries are to do with where you give of yourself to the people you have ties with, and how you participate in the give and take in the relationships you have.

Reviewing boundaries is especially important when you are living with someone or spending most of your time with them. It can be very straightforward to work this out, and the results can often startle you. More in the Mind Training box, next.

Disappointment is a lesson we all can deal with better.

A. Change what you expect from people

Consider the neighbour dispute in the chapter just read.

1. **Change the should to a could**. Commonly, expectations have a 'should' in them. 'I *could* get on with my neighbours' is better. Maybe you could, but you can't. You're not all-powerful. Accept your limitations and move on.

2. **Accept you can't control others.** Your neighbour is not going away, despite your wish. So that's that. Accept it.

3. **Lose interest in blame**. He might be to blame, you might be right. So what? It's not worked. Let go. Life isn't always fair. Remember the Life Truths, the *Akhlaaq*!

B. Review your boundaries with others

To be selfless:
Put their needs above your needs.

To respect yourself:
Put your needs above their *wants*.

You're selfish if you:
Put *your wants* before their needs.

You're a doormat if you:
Put *their wants* before your needs.

It helps to talk through relationships with a close friend or confidant, or air your concerns to Allah privately, reflecting on the matter under His gaze. It is also a direct benefit to the brain to put feelings into words. It structures your thoughts so you hear them out with your Intellect and Heart.

Use this space for your own notes on the exercise opposite.

They say if you love what you do for a living,
then it doesn't feel like work. Maybe true.

Still, all work involves interruptions and difficulties.
That's why they pay you.

Uncertainty about Skills and Passions

You might be at a crossroads where you aren't sure where your talents or skills lie. You might be reconsidering your job, or your education. The older you get, the more you realise how little there is to stop you doing anything.

Career and skills: A ready-reckoner

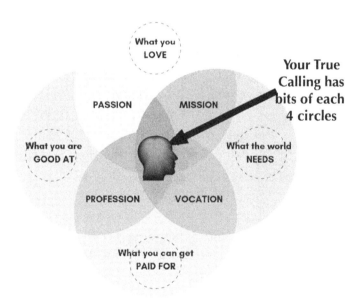

It's OK to be unsure what you want. It isn't a sign of weakness to have uncertain or multiple competing interests. It is, however, smart to put maximum reasonable effort into whatever you happen to be doing: that way, you get a sense of satisfaction, and you discover if that thing is something you could both enjoy and master long term. Hard work is its own reward.

Find a path of work or learning

Think through each circle and make a list for each.
A. What you love doing.
B. What the world needs.
C. What you are good at.
D. What you can get paid for.

Go to town. A long list, at least ten of each. Don't hold back. Add to the list over a few days, at different times of day- that way you will access different memories.

Examine what makes you feel good emotionally (serving the Nafs), and something that plays to your strengths (serving the Intellect). Then, choose which things serve both, and align with your Deen and your principles (serving the Heart). What do you find really makes you get up and go? Winning? Wealth? Helping people? Creating? Working with your hands? Feeding? Talking to others? Exploring?

Next, narrow down things that match across the four circles. Make a shortlist of 4 or 5. Not sure? Pick one, say Bismillah, and try it. You cannot know how you feel about some things until you try them. Remember to look around you and see if your activity can be partnered with someone close to you. It's useful to have allies, especially if they are in your family or close friends.

If you are genuinely stuck in your current job, then do it, accepting your position as best you can for now. Never despair about anything you are mired in. It is exactly where you need to be, to move to the next step of your life. Keep your eyes open in hope. God is there. He knows all and sees all. Call on him. He will be greatly pleased with your gentle persistence.

Use this space for your own notes on the exercise opposite.

Wishing good on others is nice.
Doing good for others
is acting with the hand of Allah.

Living in our own bubbles

A cousin of mine got frustrated with his store job. He was a very private guy, who never spoke too much to other people. A classic, brooding introvert.

Then, one day, he left his work, and took his wife and two small children to work as a volunteer for a humanitarian agency. It paid less but they gave him and his wife and children accommodation on site. They went to far off countries, got into some tricky situations, but they loved every minute of it. He's now the paid manager of a large volunteer force. He was lucky, he knew what he wanted to do. But he still took that leap of faith, praying to God with tears the nights before quitting his job. Then he happily said Bismillah and went for it.

It turned out that although he was introvert, he really wanted to be connected to other people, much more than others. He just wasn't too confident with his social skills, so he found a way to be connected by helping people by his actions.

You don't have to do anything as dramatic as him. Help out at a charity shop, a mosque volunteer force, or offering your older neighbour help with shopping and cleaning.

It is a mistake to think that because you don't feel too good, or too effective, that you must first help yourself. In fact, when we volunteer, we are helping ourselves without knowing it. It goes back to the wellbeing box.

How Volunteering Helps Your Mind

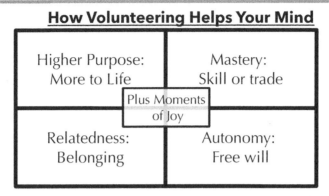

Higher Purpose: When you help someone else in need, God says it is as if you helped God himself. What a fantastic chance to add meaning to life.

Relatedness: Connecting to others is immediately apparent when you volunteer. It is a two-way pleasure.

Autonomy: You discover that you are actually capable of helping; this defeats any negative thoughts you might have about how useful or capable you are. If you can help, you have capacity to give. That means you have value to other people, and you can value yourself again.

Mastery: Giving of your trade or profession is especially valuable. It is something that other people can't do. When you give expertise, it actually improves your commitment and satisfaction from your career.

Go and do something in your local area. Find out what help is needed, and get stuck in. It may not be organised or clear; that's the nature of these opportunities. Be patient.

Use this space for your own notes on the exercise opposite.

1. Contact your masjid and ask what opportunities there are to help.

2. Find out from your local council what organisations they work with or come across in the voluntary sector.

3. Consider your skills. Can you turn them to making or doing something that is particularly helpful to a given cause?
If you are an accountant, you could do the books for a small club. If you have marketing skills, you could help promote an event. If you have wealthy contacts, you can ask them to donate. And so on.

4. Ask in your neighbourhood who might need help on a 1:1 basis for everyday things like gardening or chores, or DIY. You would be surprised at how many older people live alone. Sometimes all they would love is to talk to every couple of days.

5. Remember the most vulnerable include people with mental health crisis. Consider volunteering for a helpline service; people like the Samaritans will give you the training you need.

We cannot overcome the inevitable.
But the inevitable need not overcome us.

Negative Thoughts Running Riot

To be a positive person requires more than just blind happiness. If you are just 'happy' without any basis, you are actually quite vulnerable. It wouldn't take too much to upset you. You would probably miss signs of danger or warning too.

However, it's not common for people to be just emptily happy. It's far more common to become weighted down with miseries and insecurities. The problem is worsened because memory is *state-dependent,* meaning that if you're in a bad mood, you remember bad things more selectively.

The other problem is that your Nafs (Ego) is generally inclined to be cautious and pessimistic about uncertainty, overestimating the negative side of things. It's doing its job in protecting you, but this can get out of hand. You find yourself agreeing with emotions which are designed to warn you, but you take them as the actual truth.

These thoughts are called 'negative automatic thoughts'. To challenge them, the Muslim Mind can look at them in three ways, each focussed on its three parts. To calm the Nafs, calm the body. Do deep breathing, accept the emotions without a fight, just let them decay on their own. To use the Intellect, question the actual truth of the negative assumptions behind your feelings. And to use your Heart, remember your Deen and your highest wisdoms.

Activity Box: How to Challenge Negative Thinking

Problem thinking pattern, and example	Solution A: Acceptance of Nafs	Solution B: Look for truths with your Intellect	Solution C: Use your Heart to seek higher wisdom and faith
Black-or-white thinking *"I am a failure"*	All emotions are temporary, and exaggerated. We always over-react.	**I have succeeded at many other things.** Failure is an event, not a person	**Failure is part of the route to success.** Our job is to make effort. Success or failure is Allah's will.
Overgeneralisation *"I always get it wrong"*	As above; Use RIADH (Garden of Peace) method to calm yourself.	**You've got things right many times before.** You got it wrong this time. Doesn't mean you get it wrong always.	**Allah determines the outcome: your duty is just to make the effort as best you can.**
Selective memory *"I've never been happy"*	As above	**When I am happier I will remember better.** I have been happy before.	**Thank Allah for the blessings you have every day.** Seek three things to be thankful for, every morning.
Mind Reading *"So and so will say no when I ask him for something"*	As above	**I am not telepathic.** It is better to ask someone to see what they think.	**Ask others with optimism and faith; Allah will give you what you need if it is better for you.** Accept whatever answer you get.
Fortune telling *"I will never be happy"*	As above.	**I can't predict the future.** There will be times when I am happy.	**Allah controls the future, not you.** All misery will pass. There's benefit in both good & bad.

196

Use this space for your own notes on the exercise opposite.

Write down some unwelcome or negative thought.

- Is it associated with a bad emotion? Try the Garden of Peace. Accept that emotions can be irrational and recurrent.
- Is it factually true?
- What is an equally likely, or more likely, positive explanation?
- What would you advise someone who had such a thought?
- What does Allah have to console someone who is having a difficult time?
- Are you losing sleep or have you changed noticeably compared to a time when you weren't having this thought? If so, seek help from a doctor or counsellor.
- Consider free apps such as Woebot. It's an A.I. program which helps break down negative thoughts.

No matter what has overcome us,
We can choose at some point
to make peace with its pain.

Trouble Processing a Traumatic Event

The Muslim is told that no terrible event, no mistake, no catastrophe or loss need be a reason for permanent loss of hope. Trauma is an extreme event where fear of loss of life or severe harm is witnessed.

The paths and consequences of trauma.

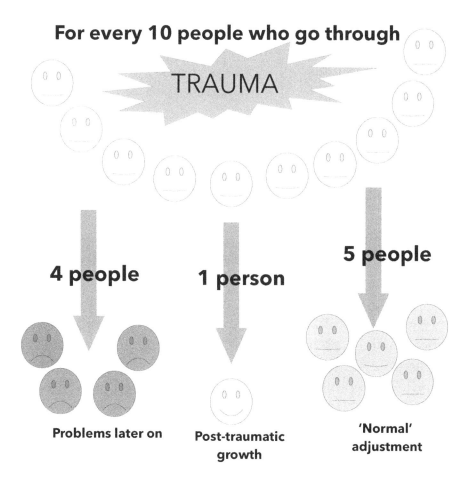

For every 10 people who go through

TRAUMA

4 people

Problems later on

1 person

Post-traumatic growth

5 people

'Normal' adjustment

For every ten people who face a significant trauma, defined as a life-threatening or similar event perceived as catastrophic:

- Four go on to develop mental health problems later on: PTSD, anxiety disorders, addiction, personality disorders and so on. They blame themselves for things they can't change.
- Five will adjust and carry on- they are resilient, having accepted that something terrible happened beyond their control, and they move on largely unchanged, if not a little wiser.
- One of them will go on to show post-traumatic growth: they go on to live life yet more fully, achieving wellbeing or success at a higher level than people who would not have gone through the same trauma.

But people tell me that bad events are psychologically damaging. How could it be that things like trauma, from a terrible car accident, can be good?

A terrible unpleasant event is a terrible unpleasant event. No Muslim wishes to face one, nor wishes it on anyone else. However, not all unpleasant events need to lead to damage.

The Muslim is told to view events, good and bad, as a chance to find, or learn, something useful. It could be as little as this: "I have survived it, therefore Allah wants me around! Alhamdulillah!"

It could be a lot bigger than that. For some people, a significant loss or terrible memory could galvanize them into finding new meaning to their life.

But what about things like Post Traumatic Stress Disorder? Are you saying that if a person gets PTSD, it's the person's fault they didn't cope with the event well?

Not at all. Again, come back to the wisdom of Allah. A mental disorder is not the person's fault: quite the opposite. They have been victims, and must be helped with all the means at their and our disposal, to become survivors and return to health. Pain need not become suffering. And once they are better, they too can find ways of growing to thrive.

What we do know is that when we look at people who survive traumas without long-term psychological problems, or indeed those uncommon folk who seem to *improve* after a trauma, we see that they tend to share certain beliefs about the world that help them. Faith is one of these things. The Muslim is instructed to believe that bad things are not to be judged as punishments or blessings: we cannot and must not read into the intentions of Allah, but just to deal with the events as they are.

The second thing that people do is consider themselves blessed. People who go through life feeling luckier, as if watched over by a benevolent force, report having greater life satisfaction, even when they go through as many bad events as others. Salah and *dhikr* (remembrance of God) are brilliant opportunities to remind ourselves that God really is watching over us very keenly, all the time. He is ever present, so we are right to believe that He will help us no matter what.

201

Within all events, there are opportunities for learning. The Muslim believes it is up to her to drill down to the valuable gold that is inside that lesson, and make use of it as a chance to improve both their faith and their functioning if this is possible.

So I am to not become emotional at all?

Not quite. Bad events can have normal psychological consequences such as anger, denial, a depressive period, and so on. This is part of recovery. Indeed, it is part of the roundedness of character that comes from growing older and wiser. Bad events can be written positively in your Heart if you choose to view them as painful but helpful lessons.

However, no trauma needs become a permanent scar on the mind's function. Problems happen when a person starts to believe that they will always be at risk from a repeat of the event, or they become depressed and hopeless on a longer term basis, or that they are somehow being targetted or punished by God. We are not to guess what God intends as such; we are only to believe he wants better for us.

Still, we are all made differently. If a Muslim has gone through some trauma and come out much worse for it, months or years later, this is not his or her fault. But it is still that Muslim's responsibility to seek help for it, and the responsibility of those around them to help them get help.

People who show post-traumatic growth are of great interest to cutting edge neuroscientists and psychologists. We are busy learning how they cope, and it turns out that we can teach a lot of this to other people. With time, the message from trauma treatment will move from survival towards revival.

Many of the ideas we now have about how to thrive as individuals come from studying these 'positive outliers'. Islam happens to have some very sturdy and sensible ways of reassuring and encouraging its believers to navigate these tests successfully.

You have a purpose, and a path. That unpleasant event was part of your path. You may not know the reason, or ever find out. Your only job is to accept it happened, and that it was hurtful. That is all.

Pain is necessary, suffering is not. Now, you have suffered something long enough. That suffering itself had a purpose, which you may never know of. Perhaps it prevented you from doing something, or being somewhere, that would have been an even greater disaster.
Accept that what God intends for you is only for the better, even if it doesn't seem so. He is wiser than you. Accept that bad things happen to good people, and vice versa. Life can, and does, seem unfair. When we accept that, we become more settled with whatever we have.

Thank God for what you do have. Take time to appreciate three good things you have that someone else does not. Imagine how life would be without those things.

Let go of guilt. You survived whatever it was, and nothing could have made it any different. Accept your fate without any fantasies. You could not have done anything to change it because it was written to happen as it did. To imagine otherwise is understandable but powerless. Let guilt and 'what-ifs' fizzle out on their own now.

Post traumatic growth (PTG)

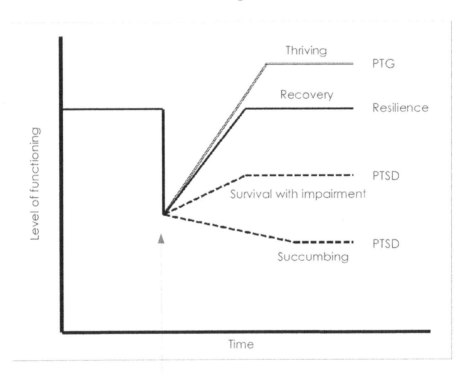

Traumatic event

Building Resilience

Internal Domain   **External domain**

Maintain
Perspective

Reach out
to others

Your Deen
Your unique strengths
Your roles and purposes
in life

Seek small
moments of joy

Be flexible and
open minded

Be optimistic
Allah will help

Accept reality

Re-interpreting a painful time

You need to see a doctor if you have any of these things:
- Re-experiencing the event as if you were there again
- Avoidance of any reminders, with numbed emotions
- Triggers which send you into a detached or very anxious state

For all other readers, do this exercise:
Identify an event in your life that caused significant distress.
a) How did it happen, and who do you blame for it?
b) Identify three feelings you felt at the time.
c) How did you cope with the stress?
d) Do you think your coping method worked?
e) Has the experience changed your life? If yes, how?

You have already survived: you've done enough. But if you like, you can also think about some ways how people re-interpret the bad things and show personal growth a more positive way. Some of those positives are listed here:

A. Relating to Others more closely
- more compassion, admit needing help, more expressive

B. New outlook, or new priorities in life
- worried less, better occupation, just get on and do things

C. Gaining a sense of personal strength
- more accepting of self, recognising your abilities

D. Becoming closer to Allah as a result of the event
- better perspective, more active in Deen, more patient

E. Appreciating Life more readily
- able to stop and reflect, take time enjoying small things

Use this space for your own notes on the exercise opposite.

**You can't control your income.
But you can always work towards a good outcome.**

Dissatisfaction With our Wealth or Status

The Prophet PBUH said
"Wealth is not in having vast riches, it is in contentment."
(Bukhari, Muslim).

The Muslim smiles because he accepts the wealth he has, no more and no less. Some faiths seem to associate poverty with being more virtuous and closer to God. They go on to say that having material things is to be viewed with great suspicion. Some go even further, encouraging complete dissociation and disposal of material things to attain a higher plane of being.

These ways of thinking offer comfort to the poor, but there are psychological problems which arise. They seem to imply that poor people are somehow more deserving of Godliness, and that rich people are somehow automatically going to find it harder to please God.

There is none of this dilemma for the Muslim. Muslims are not encouraged to favour poverty over wealth, or the other way round. Muslims are encouraged to accept that the wealth they have or gain is exactly as God intended it, and that whatever they have (or don't) is part of their particular fate. They are entitled to make their efforts to gain wealth through work and fair dealings, but there is no inherent blessing in wealth or poverty. There are stark warnings against laziness, and against hoarding of wealth though.

The Muslim knows as sure as the sky is blue:

a) Wealth is of no importance to his worth to God. Both poor and rich are equal in the eyes of God,
b) Having wealth comes with responsibilities, and
c) Being wilfully poor due to inaction or laziness is also a sin.

Wealth clearly offers luxury, protection, safety and status. These things are comforts in life. However, in what seems like a very fair deal, the wealthy Muslim has responsibilities to handle his wealth in a way which pleases Allah.

What a sensible state of affairs! Neither poor nor rich have a monopoly on God's attention, and everyone has an individual set of assets which they must accept as precisely and correctly theirs. Your responsibility is to make good on what you have given you. You strive to make the best of it, to increase it only if it is halal and wise to do so, and to spend of it wisely, ensuring that you neither hoard nor squander.

Instagram, March 2020

211

Mind Training Box: Getting wealth into perspective

Imagine you have a very wealthy friend

You are on board his luxury yacht with him and his son.

Now imagine he is very sad. He got divorced from his wife because he was never home. He feels unloved by his own mother, who is a cold and controlling company boss. She was overprotective of him as a kid. As a result, he has few friends at all. He had 'friends' who disappeared after they stole from him. Other friends seem artificial, just using him for his money. His son is sad too; unmotivated, saying he has no need to study because the family are rich.

Pick any of the Training Pages in this book.
Help them develop a plan for happiness.

What would you say to console them?
What makes for good well-being: money or character?
What does a person really need to find happiness?
How could he use they wealth to improve their well-being?

Use this space for your own notes on the exercise opposite.

**Eat food to relieve hunger, not emotions.
Those who do not find time for their bodily health
Will soon find time for illness.**

Letting our Fitness or Health slide

Everybody talks about a mind and body connection. What does it look like according to Muslims?

Good question. Have a look at this picture.

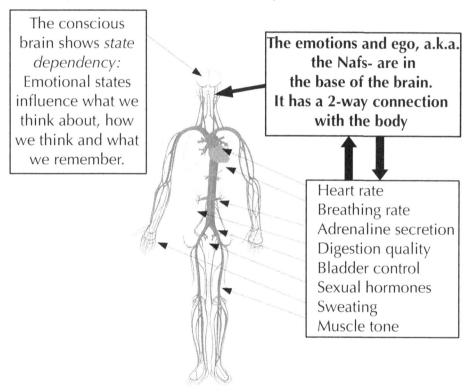

The conscious brain shows *state dependency:* Emotional states influence what we think about, how we think and what we remember.

The emotions and ego, a.k.a. the Nafs- are in the base of the brain. It has a 2-way connection with the body

Heart rate
Breathing rate
Adrenaline secretion
Digestion quality
Bladder control
Sexual hormones
Sweating
Muscle tone

The Muslim is told that the body is a vessel that is lent to him. He has a responsibility to look after it actively, maintaining a healthy weight, watching what he eats, and understanding the connection between the mind and the body.

215

Scientifically, the connection between mind and body is most easily scene when we look at how the emotional state is connected to the organs. The emotional powerhouse is also known as the Nafs. It's closest western idea is in 'emotions and Ego'.

The Muslim is taught that the Nafs is part of both his physical and mental reality. Scientifically, the Nafs occupies the whole body but its centre in the brain is at the base- where emotional and instinctive functions are located.

This part is directly connected, by nerves and hormonal links, the rest of the body, in a 2-way manner. Disturbance or activation in one causes a similar activity in the other.

So, when emotional, you notice your heart rate goes up. Your higher brain function goes down: you can't think clearly.
Your adrenal glands secrete adrenaline. Your guts feel upset or get 'butterflies' as the blood flow to them is restricted. Your muscles become twitchy. You sweat. Your breathing gets rapid and shallow.

That's fine, but how does exercise, or good diet, or even stretching the muscles, help the brain and wellbeing?

Well, you see what I just said above? It also works in reverse. To settle the emotions, you do something which is associated with a physically relaxed state. You could consciously slow your breathing down. You could stretch the muscles, reducing their tone. You could practice relaxation, where

216

you get to focus and calm your physical senses, paying them the attention they demand rather than getting overwhelmed. You could eat foods which are easier to digest. Doing any one of these things sends signals to the brain to calm down and relax.

But when I exercise, my heart speeds up, my breathing speeds up, and I sweat! And it sometimes hurts too! How could that be good for my brain?

It's a good, constructive kind of pain! I'm being flippant; let me explain it better. It's about two things.

The first is the idea of an *'energy bank'*. The energy bank in your emotional brain is usually set to 'high'. It is ready to fire off at any sign of danger. If you don't drain your energy bank, it will find ways of coming out without your consent. You get worried about insignificant things, you jump to conclusions, get annoyed easily, lose your temper or your focus, and you can't sleep. So, to tackle this issue, you drain the energy bank deliberately. You push your body by exercising, and thereby letting that steam out in a fun and stimulating way rather than letting it bounce around in your brain.

The second thing is *who's in control- you or your Nafs?* When you exercise, you certainly do cause the heart rate to go up, your breathing to quicken, and what have you. The difference is that you are doing it, you have chosen to exercise, thereby you have taken control of the system rather than let it control you. This teaches your body to be more coordinated to what you want rather than the other way round. You won't even notice the change, but you find yourself more calm, better to be around, and less easily rattled.

The Prophet PBUH was known to take exercise, running, swimming, archery and riding horses. He also ate sparingly, fasting regularly to both help his mental strength and give his gut a break.

All of this made him reportedly in very good physical state; firm of stance, broad shouldered, and physically fit, along with giving him the high amount of good judgment and endurance when he faced difficult situations. He was unafraid to put himself in a difficult position. These same options and ways are available to the modern Muslim, as models of behaviour.

Weight loss

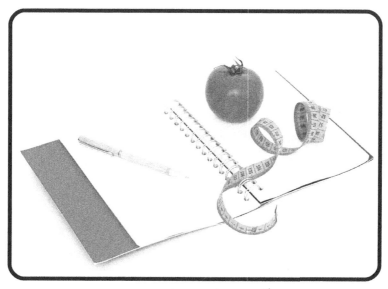

Targets and recording are VITAL

It takes 15 minutes of running to burn off the energy of one can of soda. It takes 22 minutes to burn off a single average chocolate bar.

Moral of the story?
Most weight loss is successful if we focus on our diet.
Exercise is partly helpful in improving our *fitness*, and in keeping our metabolic rate up. However, it will not burn off excess junk food unless we do many hours and hours of it!

Intermittent fasting (every few days) is a modern trend which is incredibly effective for many people. The Hadith tell us the Prophet PBUH used to fast on Mondays and Thursdays. We have had wisdom of intermittent fasting from him all along!

Principles of Physical Exercise

In Instant Insights, we talked about how Salah itself has a surprising amount of exercise. Fajr is especially helpful to get your body going.

Your chosen exercise routine depends on your level of fitness. Do something which stretches you, or gets you out of breath, but not to the point where you feel unwell.

Guidelines:
An effective exercise routine recommendation is 3 times a week, for 20 minutes each time.
Anaerobic exercise (like weights, stretching etc) helps more with your emotional processing.
Aerobic exercise (gets you out of breath) helps more with clarity of thinking.

Plans
1. Schedule a daily walk. Straight after Fajr, or before Maghreb, is best.
2. Find a partner to do any exercise with. It is the most powerful way of ensuring you keep up with a routine.
3. There are online 'live' workouts these days which you can join at scheduled times – you can work out indoors, at your level, alongside thousands of other people.
4. Consistent small effort is better than occasional 'blitzes', though if you are a 'blitzer' and can't do it otherwise, do it anyway: it's your way.
Try to enjoy the experience, or at least find it not unpleasant.

Use this space for your own notes on the exercise opposite.

Swimming, running, archery and riding horses were popular sports in the time of the Prophet PBUH, and remain so today.

Underestimating the Effect of *Iman* (Faith) on The Brain

Does Iman influence happiness?

Yes, when we check people who have Iman versus those who don't, this appears so. People with strong religious faith report higher levels of life satisfaction, more happiness day to day, and more resilience to terrible traumatic events compared to those without faith [1].

How about going to the masjid, taleem, or any other religious meeting?

When it comes to practice of faith, going to the masjid and having regular meetings based on one's faith have a direct effect on reducing risk from heart disease [2]. One study even suggested that regular religious attendance increases life expectancy by two to three years [3].

Is there a benefit on how clearly a person can think?

We have some evidence of this. One long-term study found that religious attendance reduces the decline in thinking ability that is seen in elderly people facing dementia. The authors of the study recommended religious attendance as a form of therapy[4].

How does Iman help success and contentment?

Contentment and success that comes from self control, delaying gratification, and focusing on long term goals is also increased because of having religion [5].

Is it religion that is doing this, or is it other factors like age, physical health, IQ etc?

It's religion. Studies have looked into causality- the idea that one thing directly causes another thing, rather than just 'being associated' with it, and found that there is something unique about religion that seems to benefit both mental and physical health [2].

Can we find out how religion directly influences the brain?

Yes, indeed we can.

Researchers have looked at the issue and conducted studies on religious people, comparing them to non-religious people [6]. They used scanning devices to work out which parts of the brain were active. They found that one part in particular-the Anterior Cingulate Cortex (ACC for short) gets activated when people perceive mismatches between what they know and what they see, that is, when beliefs and expectations do not match reality.

In people who believed in one God, there were two effects:

1. They got less distressed at mismatched signals which would normally cause hyperactivity in the ACC.
2. They seemed to perform better in tests which checked for errors of impulse control and coordination of different brain areas. An example is the Stroop test- look it up if you like.

Areas of the brain where religion has direct influence

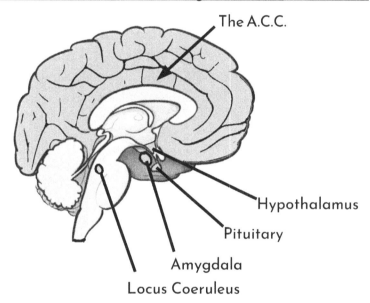

The A.C.C.

Hypothalamus

Pituitary

Amygdala

Locus Coeruleus

People of religion also seemed to have better ease and flexibility when doing tests of performance. They changed task more easily, without becoming as easily unsettled. This was independent of things like their IQ level.

In another experiment, people were observed and tested for how easily shocked or startled they were when an unexpected thing, such as a loud noise, happened.

225

They were asked to fill out a questionnaire beforehand, which included questions about how much they believed in God, and how much they believed that there was a higher control of the Universe. Religious people were consistently less startled. This shows that the influence of religion must also pervade the instinctive, unconscious areas such as the amygdala and locus coeruleus: these are where the Nafs has its seat in the brain.

Finally, in tests where the nerves and organs of the body were concerned, looking for things such as adrenaline levels, heart rate and sweating, practising religious folk were again shown to have less disturbance in those parts when stressed. The stronger their faith, the greater the calming effect.

If religious people are so much more relaxed, don't they become too easy going, unmotivated?

No. Performance and motivation are unimpaired. This is probably because religion helps one to find that 'sweet spot' where they are alert enough to do the task, but not so alert as to be overwhelmed by it. This is the 'middle' of the Yerkes Dodson curve (discussed in my last book, Instant Insights).

Is religion something as natural as any other part of our nature?

Neuroscientifically, yes, very much so. Religion is not an artificial thing to the brain. It is agreed by social anthropologists and neuroscience, that religion is a natural product of the way the human mind works. It is unique, and inseparable, from the human condition. [7]

What about all the conflicts that happen due to religion?

That's like saying car crashes are the fault of the Highway Code. Any number of things can explain this better than the idea that it is the religion itself to blame.

1. Displacement

People have wars over resources more than anything else. The wars of ancient Islam were defensive, necessitated due to the horrendous losses experienced by the Ummah at a time when Islam was very new and reviled by many. Nowadays, people who fight for a purported religious cause from any religious background seem to be using religion to deceive people into hating others. Equally often, the war is about something more material such as land, or access to wealth of some kind.

2. Fanaticism and its link to inadequacy

People with inadequately developed personality traits, who for example are vulnerable, isolated or have poor self esteem, tend to respond better to authoritarianism and being given very direct tasks. This makes them easy pickings for manipulation towards a 'cause'. In effect, their dissatisfaction with themselves becomes easily transformed into blaming others for the state of society. They get taken in easily by vengeful, remorseless or other misguided people who preach intolerant and hateful beliefs as part of their 'new mission'. They are easily radicalised, but it is not religion so much as unhealthy mind control going on.

3. Inner conflict and uncertainty in faith

For people who experience a crisis of faith, it seems that they become more distressed than even those who don't have religion. Their belief systems are always in conflict, because they cannot work out if things are under a higher power or if they have any meaning. They act out their conflict by finding reason to argue and blame others for their struggle. The most potent truth is this: Only by becoming more ensconced in the certainty of religion does the payoff of higher wellbeing arrive.

References
[1] Ellison, C.G. (1991). Religious involvement and subjective well-being. Journal of Health and Social Behaviour, 32, 80-99.

[2] Powell, L.H., Shahabi, L., & Thoresen, C.E. (2003). Religion and spirituality: Linkages to physical health. American Psychologist, 58, 36 52.

[3] Hall, D.E. (2006). Religious attendance: More cost-effective than Lipitor? Journal of the American Board of Family Medicine, 19, 103-109.

[4] Corsentino, E.A., Collins, N., Sachs-Ericsson, N., & Blazer, D. (2009). Religious attendance reduces cognitive decline among older women with high levels of depressive symptoms. Journals of Gerontology: Biological Science and Medical Sciences, 64A, 1283-1289.

[5] McCullough, M.E., & Willoughby, B.L.B. (2009). Religion, self-regulation, and self-control: Associations, explanations, and implications. Psychological Bulletin, 135, 69-93.

[6] Inzlicht, M. & Tullet, A. (2011) The need to believe: a neuroscience account of religion as a motivated process. Brain & Behavior 1, 3,192 - 251 Department of Psychology, University of Toronto, Toronto, Canada

[7] Norenzayan, A., & Shariff, A.F. (2008). The origin and evolution of religious pro-sociality. Science, 322, 58-62.

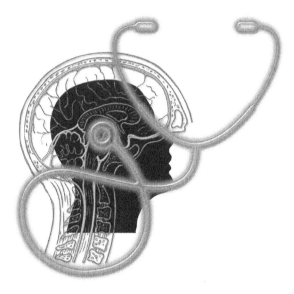

Sometimes we need a professional to help us through something beyond our control.

When Expert help should be called

This section of the book is to help those of us who might need or benefit from having expert assistance to restore our mental health.

How to know when you or someone you know could do with some help?

These signs are helpful as general indicators that something is wrong more seriously than just everyday ups and downs:

- A **significant change** in personality or behaviour which is difficult to explain or understand
- A sense that **something is going wrong** in the mind that is difficult to dismiss for the person concerned
- A sense that there is a **risk of harm** coming to oneself or others around them though their thoughts or behaviour
- **Loss of function** in some way that isn't easily explained. Memory, language, self care, awareness of surroundings
- **Marked changes in general living quality** such as self care, sleep, appetite, or mood which seem to last for more than two weeks

A walk through some common mental health problems for which help should be sought

This is by no means a comprehensive list, nor is it to be taken as evidence of a diagnosis. I have included these conditions because they have come up in my experience more frequently than most, and people ask me questions about them more than others.

Three areas are focussed on:
A. Where medical help is useful,
B. Where an Imam is useful
C Other special conditions worth mentioning

A. Where medical help is useful:

Anxiety disorders:
- A new arrival of some state of constant worry, lasting longer than a couple of weeks
- A constant worry about something specific, which can then become worry about absolutely anything
- Feeling unable to stop worrying
- A feeling like 'I'm going mad' due to lack of control over one's constant thinking
- May or may not includes themes like worry about becoming ill, or dying, or something terrible about to happened
- The worries are disproportionate to their actual chance of happening
- Physical symptoms can happen, such as frequent headaches and other pains, constant fatigue, heart

palpitations, a sense of not being able to breathe properly

- Poor concentration, irritability, and seeking reassurance a lot of the time. Preferring company.

Depression

- A new arrival, lasting at least least two weeks, of a sense of being helpless and losing hope for the future
- Feelings of guilt about the past, of being a burden to others, or that Allah is punishing the person
- A feeling of futility and total disbelief in one's own strengths.
- Changes in of sleep, appetite, and becoming disinterested in one's appearance, spouse, or friends
- Tendency to isolate oneself and be inconsolable, or seeking company more than usual. Being able to out-argue anyone who tries to offer positivity

Bipolar disorder

- Periods of depression like described above, plus:
- Alternating, or separate, periods of elevation in activity lasting a similar time.
- Not a daily or hourly alternation of mood- a common misconception- that is emotional instability, which is a separate issue.
- Agitation or elevation of mood to the point of being manic. Being unconcerned about risk, talking in a pressured way, loud, spending money or giving things away.
- Grandiosity and creativity but in a very tired-looking, chaotic sense.

Psychotic illness
- A change in behaviour and thinking, lasting more than a few days
- Losing touch with reality: believing things that are not happening, or becoming suspicious without basis
- May lose track of the senses, hearing one's thoughts out loud as if they're coming from the outside.
- Unusual or odd behaviours like sudden bouts of laughter, crying, or restlessness

Post Traumatic Stress Disorder
- At least three months after a terrible event, a person seems very poorly adjusted and somewhat terrified constantly
- Hyper-vigilance- fearing the same thing will happen again
- Re-living the same trauma as if one is going through it again and again
- Periods of dissociation, looking like one is lost in time, staring into space and emotionally numb
- Being conscious of triggers which remind of the trauma, which could start another bout of panic.

B. Situations where an Imam can be very helpful, with or without a medical professional:

Possession states
- An appearance of being 'taken over' by another entity or spirit (djinn)
- Markedly different behaviour in these times; aggression, chaotic, needy, crying, demanding
- Often accompanied by statements or accusations made toward other people, which the person would avoid making if they were 'themselves'.

Disinhibition, 'Running Amok
- Total loss of inhibition, typically hysterical in nature
- Being aggressive or provocative, with disregard for social rules which one previously respected
- Tends to happen to more than one person- a sense of being 'contagious'

Relationship Failures
- Any situation where a close couple are in deep conflict or not communication
- One party usually wants to address the issue more than the other
- Accusations or evidence of infidelity or lack of care
- Failure of Trust, failure to attend to one's role in the relationship

C. Other important conditions which are often missed and need careful evaluation:

Autism:

- Not an illness, but a lifelong condition since birth, becoming evident at around age 5 or so.
- The child doesn't speak or seem to care for eye contact. Often starts speaking in full sentences, suddenly
- Apparent shyness and not understanding social behaviour.
- Great sensitivity to sights, noises, tastes, textures or distractions
- Preferring to stick very rigidly to routines
- Great inner anxiety as the norm, even as an adult.

ADHD:

- Not an illness, but a lifelong condition since childhood although it might not be noticed until adulthood, especially in girls or bright children
- Difficulty focussing, or focussing on one thing to the expense of everything else
- Responding to novelty or challenge much more than consequences or punishment or rewards
- Tendency to be unaware of time, lose track of tasks, or attend to too many things at once without knowing which to do.
- Difficulty thinking clearly, not related to anxiety or any other issue: too many things in the mind at once, or having habitually, painfully slow thoughts.
- Knowing what to do but mostly failing to get it done.
- Very distressing and demoralising to the person.

Personality disorders
- Not illnesses, but steady states of being where someone's everyday behaviour and thinking appears bring harm to them or others.
- Often caused by traumatic upbringing.
- Personality disorders start formally in early adulthood, and can dwindle with time and therapy.
- Can include different types such as emotionally unstable, dependent and needy, antisocial or callous, or habitually angry and argumentative.
- The person often lacks insight into the situation

The list above is not designed to let the reader jump to a diagnosis. It's merely a readable, understandable description of common conditions worth mentioning to the caring reader. Do seek help if you suspect something's wrong.

The other common question is what kind of help is available? The next page gives a run-down of the types of people that are helpful for different parts of the mental health recovery or treatment process.

Remember though that **family, close friends and community are especially important.** Even if professionals step in, a person's care is greatly enhanced if their family, their close friends, and even their employer take an interest and role in helping them. Mental illness can be a tragically lonely journey. Allah has said that if we help one of his servants, it is as if we have helped Allah himself. What a grand invitation to do something that Allah loves of us: caring for one another.

PROFESSIONALS WHO HELP WITH MENTAL HEALTH

People	Their role	Typical issues they help with
Support Worker	**Paid or volunteer. Not usually qualified** in mental health formally. May or may not be in training towards higher qualification. Help with everyday issues like chats, shopping or getting organised.	*Support with* Grief Recovery from Illness Day to day life Long term conditions
Counsellor	**Listen to people and support them** in the community. Can work as part of a charity or in a paid role. Usually not formally qualified but has had some training. Can't diagnose or prescribe. Often very helpful in 'reframing' a person's problems or just listening.	*Adjustment to* Grief Loss Crisis Relationships
Imams	**Listen to issues and provide crucial knowledge** and support on spiritual and psychological matters. Can be crucial or central for many people. Communicates or co-ordinates with doctors or other professionals if appropriate.	*Support, Intervene & Guide* Spiritual matters Relationships Possessions Evil Eye Impulsivity
Family Doctors/ GPs	**First port of call for all illnesses, physical or mental.** They treat 80% of mental health issues. Some GPs are dismissive, or not confident about mental health: You MUST ask to see another, politely, or feel free to switch GP to another.	*Diagnose, Prescribe, Review, Cordinate Refer onward* Depression, anxiety, OCD, dementia, long term psychosis

238

Clinical Psycholgist & Psychother -apist	**Degree-level registered specialists** Must have a Degree in psychology or formal qualification in psychotherapy. Uses non- drug interventions. Usually registered with a national body e.g. In the UK, the UKCP and BACP. *Check online.* Many work privately &don't need a referral.	*Take on, assess, & talk-treat patient referred for:* Any appropriate mental health condition. From phobias to severe psychosis.
Social workers	**Qualified, registered professionals** who help people with all the social aspects of life, such as family care, housing, day to day support, coordinating home support. Called upon if involuntary admission is required ('sectioning') Can also do talking therapies.	*Assess, organise, intervene* Long term illness Sudden illnesses Child&Carer suppt, housing, education, employment, addiction
Psychiatric Nurses	**Nurses** who specialise in helping people with mental health. Qualified and experienced in this. Can work independently. Most work as part of a unit in the GP practice or a specialist psychiatric team.	*Support intensively, intervene, deliver treatment* Any mental health condition.
Other professions	Educational psychologists, Drama, Occupational &Art Therapists,	*Depending on the need*
Psychiatrist	**Medical doctors** specialising in mental health. Can use any treatment. Must have a medical degree and further qualifications. Some specialise in children, adults, addiction etc. Some do see patients without a referral.Can work alone of part of a team based in hospital/ community	*Receive, diagnose, prescribe, talk, coordinate, assess risk, +/- involve other specialists:* Any mental health condition.

239

End of book. May Allah bless and help the reader and all humanity to find a happy, virtuous and contented life, Ameen. There is No Deity but Allah, and the Prophet Muhammad is His Messenger.

Dr TK Harris, MD,
April 2020/ Sha'baan 1441

'Alhamdulillah'

More works by Dr Harris: Search for 'Instant Insights' in paperback or E-book, and soon in audiobook format.
Email him on drtkharris@gmail.com
Instagram @drtkharris
Blog – **drtkharris.wordpress.com** Always updated with free articles and new material.

Coming Soon, Inshallah:
- Youtube Channel
- Instant Insights The App

INDEX